REVISED AND UPDATE

HOW TO HELP YOUR CHILD

WITH

HOMEWORK

Every caring parent's guide to encouraging good study habits and ending the Homework Wars

FOR PARENTS OF CHILDREN AGES 6–13

Marguerite Cogorno Radencich, Ph.D. and Jeanne Shay Schumm, Ph.D.

Edited by Pamela Espeland

free spirit
PUBLiSHiNG®

Works
for kids™

Library of Congress Cataloging-in-Publication Data

Radencich, Marguerite C., 1952–1998
How to help your child with homework : every caring parent's guide to encourag-ing good study habits and ending the homework wars : for parents of children ages 6–13 / by Marguerite C. Radencich and Jeanne Shay Schumm : edited by Pamela Espeland. — Rev. ed.
p.   cm.
Includes bibliographical references and index.
ISBN 1-57542-006-6 (pbk.)
1. Homework. 2. Education—Parent participation—United States.
I. Schumm, Jeanne Shay, 1947– . II. Espeland, Pamela.
III. Title.
LB1048.R22   1997
649'.68—dc20   96-16097
                                                      CIP

10 9 8 7 6 5 4
Printed in the United States of America
Cover and book design by MacLean & Tuminelly
Illustrations by Caroline Price
Index prepared by Eileen Quam and Theresa Wolner

Free Spirit Publishing Inc.
400 First Avenue North, Suite 616
Minneapolis, MN 55401-1724
(612) 338-2068
help4kids@freespirit.com
www.freespirit.com

Dedication

To Diana Lia, Nicholas, Christina, Daniel, David, and Benjamin
MCR

To Jerry and Jamie
JSS

Contents

List of Reproducible Pages

Introduction

"I didn't do my homework because you forgot to remind me."

"I didn't do my homework because my parents came home late from work."

"I did my homework but the hard drive crashed."

"I did my homework but I left it on the bus."

"I did my homework but it was stolen from my locker."

"I did my homework but my baby sister wrecked it."

"I did my homework but the dog ate it."

"I left my homework in my pocket and my mom put my jeans in the wash."

Teachers have heard excuses like these since the first teacher made the first homework assignment. As long as teachers keep giving homework, students will keep trying to get out of doing it.

Because we are teachers and tutors, we are often asked by our friends, relatives, neighbors, and the parents of our students for advice on handling the homework issue. (One of us has also been on the other side, having brought up a child through public and private schools.) Because we are researchers, we have tried to find answers. We spoke with other educators and came away with ideas and suggestions. We spoke with parents to discover what they had tried and what had been successful for them.

The first edition of *How to Help Your Child with Homework* was well-received, even winning awards. We were led to this second edition because of 1) the continuing success of the first edition, 2) our desire to provide the most up-to-date information on how technology and changes in the field of education are affecting homework, and 3) our wish to share new ideas on the subject.

Why do teachers bother with homework? Why do they continue to inflict homework on kids, their parents, and themselves? In fact, there are several excellent reasons:

▶ Homework encourages children to practice skills they haven't yet fully learned.

▶ Homework gives children opportunities to review skills they might otherwise forget.

▶ Homework enriches and broadens a child's knowledge.

▶ Homework teaches responsibility.

▶ Homework allows for tasks which are too time-consuming to be finished during school hours.

As a parent, you can probably think of a few more reasons yourself. You may remember times from your own childhood when a homework assignment made the difference between fully understanding a subject or barely grasping it, between excelling on a test and just scraping by. There may have been occasions when you actually *enjoyed* doing your homework—when you sat at the kitchen table or sprawled on the living room floor, working at your own pace on a project that fascinated you, without the distractions of the class-room.

For many parents engaged in the Homework Wars, the obvious strategy is to look back at their own experiences as children and draw from them. Unfortunately, this seldom produces workable solutions. Schools today are different than they were back then. Recent decades have seen dramatic changes in family makeup, in the pressures being put on kids to succeed at earlier ages, and in the way school subjects are taught.

Just as some of our parents suffered when the "new math" was introduced during the 1960s, parents today are amazed by how quickly children surpass our own computer literacy. We're confused by the modern approach to master-ing writing skills, which requires children to correct grammar and punctuation errors only on revisions and not on first drafts. We feel out of touch with the changes in curriculum and the burgeoning amounts of information our chil-dren are given to learn. We wonder if we can keep up.

Regardless of what parents know or don't know (or think they don't know), most are still eminently capable of helping their children with home-work. You don't have to be an expert in every subject. You don't have to be up-to-date on the latest teaching methods. All you have to be is caring, con-cerned, and willing to spend some time with your child (or children).

We're not talking about hours every day from now through high school graduation. This book stresses the teaching of *study skills*, which children don't always learn in school. As your children learn these skills from you, they will, in effect, be learning how to learn on their own. We predict that the more time you spend teaching these skills today, the less you'll have to spend in the future—and the more independent your children will become.

Homework doesn't have to be unpleasant. It *shouldn't* be unpleasant. It may not be as much fun as playing or watching TV, but there's no rule that says it has to be pure, unrelieved torture. At the very least, it ought to be bearable, for you as well as your child. This book offers specific strategies, tips, and techniques that can make homework more bearable—and even enjoyable—for everyone concerned. They have worked for other families, and they can work for you.

Recent educational research has shown that *when parents become involved in their children's schoolwork, children do better in school.* They become more effective learners, and they become more willing learners. By deciding to help your child with homework, you will do more than end the Homework Wars. You will give your child the tools he or she needs to succeed.

Marguerite Cogorno Radencich

Jeanne Shay Schumm

Getting Started

"It is not what you do for your children
but what you have taught them to do for themselves
that will make them successful human beings."

Ann Landers

The two-way street between home and school

It goes without saying that the better your relationship is with your child's teacher and school, the more successful your child's school experience will be. Because homework is part of your child's school experience, it's wise to make that relationship a two-way street. Following are some suggestions for accomplishing this.

Talk to your child about school.

Ask your child to tell you about what happens during the day. What does your child like best about school? What does she like least about it? The more you know, the more prepared you'll be if problems arise.

Plan to meet with your child's teacher at least three times during the school year.

Communicate your willingness to cooperate with the teacher. Don't wait for a personal invitation; an Open House (most schools hold them annually) is an excellent opportunity to have a *brief* conversation. If you need more time, make an appointment.

Learn about the homework policy for the school district, school, and class.

Some school districts have homework policies that schools and individual teachers are required to follow. In other districts, individual schools and/or teachers are responsible for setting their own homework policies. Find out about the policies that affect your child. Ask how often homework is assigned, when it is assigned, and how homework will affect your child's grade.

Learn about the curriculum at your child's school.

What is your child being taught? How is she being taught? Many schools provide parents with written summaries of the curriculum. In other schools, teachers describe the curriculum during parent meetings or open houses. Ask whether this information is provided as a matter of course; if it isn't, tell the teacher that you'd appreciate having it. Learn about what your child is learning.

Find out how you will be informed about your child's progress.

Will children bring papers home on a weekly basis? Will there be interim reports between report cards? Some schools are now using portfolios—folders or binders that include samples of children's work and summary sheets that indicate their progress throughout the year. Ask if your child's teacher is compiling or plans to compile an assessment portfolio for your child.

Act quickly if you suspect that a problem exists.

Tell the teacher that you want to meet, and make an appointment as soon as possible. Don't just show up unannounced! Spur-of-the-moment conferences translate into incomplete information. They aren't fair to you, the teacher, or your child.

Sometimes a teacher will notice a problem before the parents do. Typically, a teacher will initiate communication by sending a note home with the child. Be sure to respond, either with a phone call or with a note of your own. Depending on the nature of the problem, you may want to schedule a conference to discuss it.

If your child is having difficulties doing schoolwork, make sure there are no hidden physical causes. A visit to your pediatrician, ophthalmologist, or audiologist can uncover any that might exist.

How much homework is enough?

How can you tell if your child is getting the right amount of homework? First, it helps to understand that homework policies differ widely from state to state, school to school, and teacher to teacher. Typically, the amount of homework increases as the child moves up to higher grades.

▸ If your child consistently tells you that he has no homework or has "done it on the bus," check with the teacher. If what your child is saying is true, the teacher might be willing to assign more homework or more difficult homework.

▸ If your child's homework load allows no time for play, check with the teacher. The homework load might be excessive. Discuss this possibility with the teacher and try to work out a solution together.

Between these two extremes, it's sometimes difficult to figure out what constitutes an "appropriate" homework load. Some children take longer than others to complete assignments; also, the homework load may be heavier or lighter at certain times of the year. *In our opinion, appropriate averages are 30 minutes of homework a day for first graders and 90 minutes a day for sixth graders,* with proportional amounts assigned to the grades between. Some educators recommend more homework, while others feel that the school day is long enough and any amount of homework is too much. If you are in total disagreement with the policy followed by your child's teacher or school, schedule a conference and try to reach a compromise.

How can you tell if the content of your child's homework is appropriate? Here's a good rule of thumb: *Homework should not involve anything that is brand-new to the child.* If your child consistently requires a lot of help with homework, schedule a conference with the teacher. Possible problems may include:

▸ Your child may not be paying attention in class.

▸ Your child may have a listening or memory problem and may not be learning what is taught in class.

▸ Your child may be using homework as a way to get your attention.

▸ Your child's teacher may be assigning work that has not yet been taught in class.

▸ The assignments may be unclear, unfair, or without purpose.

Once you identify the problem, you and the teacher can work together toward a solution. Keep in mind that most teachers really *want* to help their students. If you maintain a positive attitude, most problems can be solved at the classroom level.

 **HELP!**

"My son's teacher requires him to do homework, but she never grades it. For example, every week he has to look up 15 words in a dictionary and copy the definitions. But as far as I can tell, the teacher just puts a check in her grade book that my son did the homework, but doesn't grade it at all. Is this sound educational practice?"

Research indicates that homework is most effective when teachers grade it and give students feedback about it. If homework is just busy work, it serves no real purpose. Talk to your son's teacher. Perhaps she reviews homework with the students in class. Or maybe she doesn't grade specific assignments but monitors her students' performance on homework in another way. If neither seems to be the case in your son's class, ask the teacher how your son (and you) can get more feedback on the work he does at home.

"My daughter usually understands her homework, but she finishes it too quickly and makes a lot of mistakes."

Check her homework after she completes it and have her make the necessary corrections. Limit your help to general suggestions for improvement. (*Examples*: "You've forgotten two periods in this paragraph. Find where they belong." Or "Five of your math problems seem to be wrong. Check your answers.") Another alternative is to block off a specific amount of time each day as a homework period. If your daughter finishes her homework before the end of the period, let her spend the rest of the time on schoolwork-related activities you give to her. Finally, you might consider starting a "reward system" for neat and accurate work.

"My son is in the fifth grade. His school decided to 'departmentalize' this year. In other words, he now has different teachers for math, language arts, science, and social studies. The idea behind the departmentalization is to help get the children ready for middle school, but from my point of view, it's a disaster! My son can't keep track of his homework assignments from class to class, and he never seems to know when he's going to have a test. All of this switching around is very confusing to him—and to me!"

Set up a meeting with your son's teachers right away—don't delay. Request that all four teachers be present (perhaps you can schedule a meeting on a teacher planning day). Explain the situation and suggest that you all put your heads together on an action plan. Work with the teachers to develop a system for monitoring the plan and making certain that your son is keeping up with homework and tests. (Perhaps your son can keep one assignment sheet for all classes; see pages 154 and 155 for examples you can copy and use.) Once you decide on a plan with the teachers, let your son know what it is. Be patient; it may take some time before the plan becomes routine and all of the bugs are worked out.

Who should help with homework?

Many parents feel that they don't have the skills to help their children with homework. In fact, research has shown that the *quality* of the parent-child interaction is more important than the actual techniques used. You might be surprised at what a good teacher you can be!

But helping with homework doesn't have to be solely your responsibility as a parent. You may discover that more than one family member is willing and able to lend a hand. As you decide who should help your child with homework, consider these questions:

▶ Is there someone in your family who's a "natural teacher"? Maybe it's a parent. Or maybe it's a sibling or other relative who lives nearby and is willing to help.

▶ Is there someone in your family who's especially knowledgeable about or talented in a particular subject area? Maybe Dad studied French in college. Maybe big sister is a math whiz.

You might also look beyond your immediate family. If your child spends the after-school hours with a sitter, perhaps the sitter can help. Or maybe the sitter you regularly call for weekday or weekend evenings can lend a hand. And don't forget about other children your child knows. Kids who study with friends can help each other; one of our sisters studied for years with a neighbor. For the sake of simplicity, this book is written to the parent and assumes that the parent is the one who will most likely be involved. But that doesn't have to be the case. Ask around and you may find that help is available from other sources.

Of course, you should exercise good judgment in any of these arrangements. Make sure that the person really wants to help and understands this basic principle: *Homework should never be done for the child.* Also make sure that he or she has the time. Helping with homework should not put an excessive burden on anyone, particularly siblings. If big brother has an especially busy school and social schedule, the added responsibility may not be beneficial to him or to the child in need of assistance.

Why and how to set a homework schedule

Children (and adults) respond well to structure and consistency. We all feel more secure when we know what to expect. (If you need convincing, think back to how you felt on your child's first day of kindergarten, compared to how you feel now when your child leaves for school.) This sense of security is the main reason for setting a firm schedule for homework sessions. Another good reason is that this eliminates one of the most common battles in the Homework Wars: arguing about when to do it. Finally, setting a schedule ensures that homework will get done by a reasonable hour. Many children are natural procrastinators; if we let them, they'll put off starting their homework (or any other chore) until the last possible minute—or they won't do it at all.

You may be blessed with a child who does her homework without prodding or reminding. If this is the case, she should be allowed to set her own schedule, with only occasional monitoring from you. However, it's far more likely that you will need to get directly involved in this process. In deciding when your child's homework sessions should be scheduled, keep these guidelines in mind:

> ▶ Most kids need some time to unwind after school and before settling in to do their homework—but they shouldn't wait until it's so late that they're too tired to complete it effectively.

> ▶ Children have trouble concentrating when they're hungry. If homework must be done before dinner, offer a healthy snack. (Please, no sugary snacks or caffeinated soft drinks.)

> ▶ Younger children have a harder time sitting still for extended periods than older children. Fortunately, short study sessions often lead to more learning than longer ones. For example, it's better to practice flash cards for two 10-minute sessions than one 20-minute marathon.

Most families already have their own schedules—times when people arrive home from school and work, times when they sit down to dinner, times when the kids go to sports or scouts. Although it will almost certainly be a challenge, try to fit homework in when it will be least disruptive. On the other hand, homework should be a priority, and it should be taken seriously. We can't tell you the best place to fit it in because we don't know your family's situation. But we *can* reassure you that once you set a schedule and stick to it, it *does* get easier. And once your child gets used to the idea that homework will be done no matter what, you can afford to be flexible when the need arises.

Homework Schedule

PREPARED FOR: *Johnny*   PREPARED BY: m♡m (xoxo)

4:00-4:30	After school play time.
4:30-5:30	Start homework. FIRST, figure out what you need to do. NEXT, decide which things you want me to help you with. (Do HARDEST homework first!)
5:30-6:00	Stop homework. Play time.
6:00-7:00	Dinner.
7:00-7:30	Finish any leftover homework.
7:30-8:30	Play or TV time (IF HOMEWORK IS DONE). Check with me BEFORE turning on the TV!
8:30	Bedtime.

There is one issue that may need addressing in advance: the problem of what we call the Overprogrammed Child. Parents naturally want their children to have everything. However, the child who has karate classes on Mondays, piano lessons on Tuesdays and Thursdays, and scouts on Wednesdays may simply be doing too much. Kids need time for homework and chores, and they also need free time for play. If your child is involved in a variety of activities, you may want to reassess the situation—especially if her grades are suffering, or there are signs of emerging emotional difficulties. A few signs to watch for include:

- refusing to go to school or talk about school
- refusing to do homework, and/or
- physical ailments with no identifiable medical cause.

If your child shows any of these signs, or if you have other reasons to believe that your child may be overprogrammed, then one or more of these extracurricular activities should be stopped.

After you have determined a specific time (or times) for homework sessions, you're ready for the next step: determining how that time should be organized. Here are some parent-tested recommendations:

1. Encourage your child to start each homework session by looking over everything that needs to be done. Ask, "Which parts can you do on your own? Which parts will you need help with?"

2. Suggest that your child do the most difficult or distasteful task first, before fatigue sets in. There's nothing worse than being asked to explain a complicated math problem when both you and your child are ready to call it a day.

3. When homework involves memorizing information or reviewing for a test, this should be done early in the session, while both you and your child are fresh. Then, at the end of the session, go over the material one more time. If possible, you may want to review it again in the morning before school.

 **HELP!**

"I get home from work just in time to fix dinner. My daughter has gymnastics after school and eats dinner as soon as she gets home. Both of us are exhausted afterward. How can we possibly fit homework in?"

Your case is an exception to our "do-the-hardest-homework-first" rule. You may want to try letting your daughter do her easiest homework in the evening, before bedtime. Then, depending on how much homework she has, have her get up half an hour earlier in the morning, dress and eat breakfast, and complete the more difficult work before leaving for school.

"My son does his homework as long as there isn't anything interesting on TV. If there is, I have to nag him to do it."

What's wrong with exercising some parental control? Decide on a specific number of hours per day (preferably *one* at the most) during which your son is allowed to watch television. Have him tell you which programs he wants to watch, and either give your approval or suggest something else. And make it a rule that if he really wants to watch his programs, he has to finish his homework first. He'll probably scream and yell and argue, but stand firm; once he learns that you mean business, he'll settle down—and buckle down.

"My son does his daily assignments without any problem. But he always wants to stay home from school on days when reports or special projects are due."

That's probably because he's not prepared. He needs help budgeting time for long-term assignments. Start by doing some "backwards planning"; use a calendar and count back from the day a project is due to determine how much time he has. Then work together on a "project plan." For suggestions, see pages 114–116.

How to set up a home study center

One of us grew up with three brothers and sisters. Everyone had a special place for doing homework. One claimed the dining room table, another retreated to our parents' study, and the other two worked in their bedrooms.

Deciding *where* your child should do homework is as important as deciding *when* it should be done. Learning styles differ from child to child, and the study center should allow for these differences. Some points to consider include:

Lighting

Good lighting is always important, but some children prefer brighter lights than others. Any child with his own desk should have a desk lamp.

Seating

Good posture helps concentration. This isn't to say that your child can't slump into a beanbag chair to read a story, but for optimum attention to homework, a straight-backed chair at a table or desk is best.

Noise

Although some children can study in the midst of TVs and radios blaring, other children playing, dogs barking, and parents conversing, it's better if the study center is relatively quiet. If possible, it should be located away from where distracting toys are kept. A "Do Not Disturb" sign can be a nice touch.

Study materials

Often the first few minutes of homework time are wasted as children search the house for materials they need. You can put an end to this by stocking the home study center with writing instruments, erasers, paper, note cards, paper clips, pencil sharpeners, correction fluid, and other supplies. Make a small chalkboard or slate available for exercises that would normally be done on scratch paper, and hang a bulletin board for posting calendars, important notices, and directions for special projects.

A computer

Home computers are becoming as common in the United States as television sets. Computers are helpful for accessing information for reports and projects, completing writing assignments, and practicing basic skills in reading and mathematics. If you decide to include a computer in your child's home study center (or if you allow him to use the family computer), you'll also need supplies such as printer paper, blank diskettes, and computer software. See Chapter 8 for more detailed information about homework and computers.

Reference materials

The study center should include a small reference library. For children in first grade, we suggest a "pictionary," or picture dictionary. For children above first grade level, supply a dictionary written at a level your child can understand. Check your local bookstore; good dictionaries for students are published by HarperCollins, Houghton Mifflin, Simon & Schuster, and Merriam Webster. You might also want to select a thesaurus for your child; HarperCollins, Simon & Schuster, and Troll Associates all publish student thesauruses we recommend. A set of encyclopedias saves trips to the library; the *World Book* is an excellent resource for older elementary school children, since it's easier to read than most other encyclopedias. An atlas and a globe can also be useful.

If you have a computer in your home, consider purchasing an encyclopedia or dictionary on diskette or CD-ROM. Multimedia reference works are becoming more readily available (and affordable); interactive encyclopedias and video almanacs can bring learning to life for your child. If you subscribe to an online service such as Prodigy, CompuServe, or America Online (or if you have a direct Internet connection), encyclopedias, dictionaries, almanacs, and other searchable reference materials are easily accessible.

Your presence

Generally speaking, the younger the child, the more likely it is that he will get down to work if you're nearby. You shouldn't have to hover over him during every homework session, but if he's at the kitchen table while you're preparing dinner, or at the dining room table while you're reading the newspaper in the next room, the opportunities for distraction will be fewer. And you'll be around to answer questions and provide encouragement. Older children with a proven track record of doing their homework without constant supervision can be allowed to study in their room or another place of their choosing, as long as it meets the criteria outlined above.

20 tips for homework helpers

1. Maintain two-way communication with your child.

Don't just lecture. Listen and respond to what your child has to say. When you respond, don't plead or argue. (Pleading puts your child in charge; arguing creates a no-win situation.) Instead, respond assertively and positively.

2. Don't give your child a choice unless you mean it.

Instead of saying, "Would you like to work on your science homework now?" say, "It's time to work on your science homework. Please join me at the table." Or, if you really want to offer a choice between two tasks, phrase it in a way that's likely to get the desired response. *Example*: "You can either do your science homework now or after dinner. But if you wait until after dinner, you won't be able to watch your favorite TV program."

3. Set goals with, not for, your child. Then focus on one at a time.

Start with a goal that your child is almost guaranteed to achieve. That will make the others more appealing and continued success more likely.

4. Expect progress.

We all respond to the expectations other people have of us. (This is known as the self-fulfilling prophecy syndrome.) If your expectations are low, your child's achievements are likely to match them. If your expectations are high *but not unreasonable,* your child will respond in kind.

5. Make your child aware of his or her improvement. Reward achievement.

Don't "pay" for every accomplishment with a treat or a promise. Often it's enough simply to say, "You did a really good job on that map. I'm proud of you." But if your child works especially hard on a challenging assignment and completes it successfully, that's worth celebrating.

6. Praise generously, yet honestly.

Praise will lose its effectiveness if used indiscriminately, plus a child can usually tell when you're not being sincere.

7. Direct praise to the task at hand.

Saying, "You spelled eight out of ten words right. Much better!" is more specific than "Good for you!" Specific praise guides future behavior.

8. Try not to show disappointment if your child doesn't do as well as you'd like.

Look for your child's strengths; avoid criticism. The child whose performance is poor doesn't need reminding; she needs encouragement and reassurance that you value her *regardless of her performance.*

9. Be enthusiastic. Use humor.

Starting every homework session with the *Star Wars* theme might be going overboard. But it doesn't hurt to smile and say, "I like spending this time with you." And you don't have to be deadly serious about it. Laughter, shared jokes, and even a tickle or two can go a long way toward lightening the homework load.

10. Use timers and competition wisely.

For some children, a timer spurs effort and puts an end to stalling; for others, it's anxiety-producing. If the latter seems true for your child, put the timer away. Some children enjoy competing against themselves and trying to better their past achievements, and if this is the case with your child, that's fine. But competition with friends, brothers, or sisters can be threatening and debilitating, especially if the child is at an academic disadvantage.

11. Be prepared to teach.

Even though the teacher is responsible for teaching the subject matter, this doesn't always happen, and you may need to "fill in the blanks." Skimming the textbook and carefully reading lesson materials and handouts will prepare you for this role.

12. Use concrete, hands-on materials whenever possible, especially (but not exclusively) when working with a young child.

For example, it's easier to learn 2 + 3 with blocks than with pictures. And it's easier to learn with pictures than with numbers.

13. Help your child build associations between what he or she already knows and what is being learned.

Children learn new concepts by learning how they are like and different from concepts they already know. *Examples:* "Multiplying fractions is like regular multiplying except. . . ." "A stream is like the canal behind Grandma's house except. . . ." "The electrons in an atom circle the proton. What circles the sun?" A child who mentally pictures the solar system has a better understanding of what goes on in an atom.

14. Provide adequate practice.

Children shouldn't just learn material; they should actually *overlearn* it to promote the development of long-term memory. Try to ignore complaints of "We already did that! This is boring!" But don't run a subject or a concept into the ground. Know when to stop.

15. Provide variety.

If a child starts fidgeting excessively over a math book, switch to spelling for a while. Return to math later. In between, share a snack, take a short walk, or have a joke-telling session.

16. Encourage creativity.

Although you should be careful about "sticking to the rules," a certain amount of creativity can "help the medicine go down." A story in one of the basal readers (reading textbooks) tells of a child whose Thanksgiving homework assignment was to make a Pilgrim doll. The child's mother was an Eastern European immigrant. The child dressed the doll in Russian attire, and the doll served as a lesson to the class that the United States has had many kinds of pilgrims over the years.

17. Encourage independence.

For example, if your child is able to read directions independently, encourage her to do so.

18. Take every opportunity to build your child's self-esteem.

This includes, but isn't confined to, most of the other tips already presented here. Use your imagination and your natural affection and concern to think of other ways to show your child that she is a worthwhile and important person.

19. Check with the teacher before correcting your child's homework.

Many teachers want to see a student's mistakes; they use them to determine where more teaching is called for. A perfect parent-corrected paper can be misleading and can rob a child of the extra help she may need.

20. Show a positive attitude toward school.

If you have problems with your child's school or teacher, don't discuss them with the child. Instead, show your respect for school by emphasizing the importance of regular attendance, a neat appearance, and grades that reflect your child's true capabilities. Then make an appointment to speak privately with the teacher.

Troubleshooting

"You cannot put the same shoe on every foot."

Publilius Syrus

If you have difficulties working with your child. . .

Experience has already shown you that parenting isn't easy. Whenever you make a change in the way you relate to your child, you can expect problems to surface at some point along the way. Deciding to help with homework will change the way you relate to your child. He may resist your help at first—or accept it initially and resist it later. Your best-laid plans may founder on the realities of temper tantrums and power struggles.

What can you do if you have difficulties working with your child? First, try not to assume that any and all homework-related problems are the fault of your child, the teacher, or the school. A surprising number may trace back to *your own* experiences and behaviors. There's nothing unusual about this; even parents aren't perfect! The point is, these problems *can* be solved. All it takes is willingness on your part to examine your expectations and behaviors and modify those that get in the way.

Remind yourself of these simple yet essential truths: You are an adult; your child is still a child. You have years of experience to draw on; your child is relatively new to the world. You are capable of problem-solving, analyzing, and reasoning; your child may not yet have developed these skills. Also, your child is counting on you to be older and wiser, to set rules and boundaries, and to offer guidance when and where it's needed. Often the more a child rebels and resists, the more that child is crying out for parents to take charge. When you say, "You *will* do your homework, and that's final," you're not being mean or unfair—you're being a parent! And the more firm and consistent you are, the easier it will become and the more responsive your child will be.

As we talk with parents about difficulties they have in working with their children, the following issues come up again and again. Exploring them here may help you to avoid them or deal with them effectively should they arise.

"My parents never had trouble getting me to do my homework. I can't understand why my child is so stubborn about it."

Are you treating your child the way your parents treated you? There are two reasons why this may be backfiring: You aren't your parents, and your child isn't you.

Even though most parents vow that they will never treat their children as their parents treated them, research has shown that we tend to repeat our parents' behaviors. It's perfectly fine to draw on the wisdom you gained from your mother and father—as long as you also leave room for your own good sense and instincts. And keep an open mind to what today's experts are saying about how children learn. Much of this information was unavailable to our parents, and we can all stand to benefit from it. For suggestions on books you may want to read, see pages 147–148.

"I don't have any trouble working with other people's children. Why is it so hard with mine?"

Many parents can do a good job of teaching children—as long as they're not their own. There are many reasons for this. To begin with, you're usually not as emotionally attached to other people's children. Your expectations aren't as high. Your ego isn't as involved.

When working with your own child, you may find it hard to maintain a balance between being interested and being pushy. We all want to encourage our children to do their best. It's an almost irresistible parental urge. But it's far more effective to be genuinely *interested* in what they are doing, what they are experiencing, what they are feeling, and what their needs are. Being interested means putting them first, listening to what they have to say, and tailoring your responses to what's best for them.

You may discover that your emotions interfere with your teaching. While honesty is usually the best policy, there are times when it's best to conceal your true feelings for the sake of your child's self-esteem. For example, no child functions well in the face of parental disappointment or anger. Rather than show these feelings, take a break. Go off by yourself to cool down, or do something fun with your child. You'll both feel better.

Take time to examine your goals for your child. Do you see your child as an extension of yourself? Do you see your child as a reflection of your parenting abilities? Do you want your child to achieve everything you didn't or couldn't achieve when you were in school? Are you subconsciously trying to "keep up with the Joneses" through your child's accomplishments? Remember that your child is a unique individual—one of a kind, and one in a million. The more you project this attitude, the more your child may achieve. The freedom to be oneself is a powerful motivator.

"I must have gone over this material a thousand times! Why can't my child get it?"

Many parents have told us, "I don't know how you do it. I'd never have the patience to be a teacher." So you didn't become a teacher—and here you are, forced to teach anyway! If it's any consolation, even the best teachers get impatient. As long as you recognize your impatience and can deal with it effectively, don't let it concern you. It's normal, natural, and inevitable.

The only time to worry is when your lack of patience (or your emotional involvement, expectations, or ego) seriously hampers your ability to help your child. If it becomes clear to you that you're *not* the best person for the job, find someone else. Many parents hire professional tutors for their children. (For more on this topic, see pages 30–32.)

"I work crazy hours and can't always supervise my child's homework."

If your child needs homework supervision and no one is available to provide it in your place, you'll need to make an alternate plan. Call or visit your child's teacher, explain your situation, and ask for suggestions. It's possible to provide supervision under all kinds of circumstances; it just takes some planning. We know of one case where a father shocked his son by checking up on him from Mexico!

How to help your child keep track of assignments

All homework starts life as an assignment, given by a teacher to a child. Unfortunately, many assignments get lost, misplaced, or misunderstood somewhere between school and home. Unless you live in the Bermuda Triangle, there's really no reason why assignments can't arrive home in the same condition they left school. All it takes is a few new habits—and a few useful organization tools.

A bookbag

A bookbag is an absolute must where homework is concerned. Your child's bookbag should be prepared every night before school and left in a convenient, regular place for pickup in the morning.

Shopping for a bookbag can be an enjoyable parent-child outing. As much as possible, respect your child's wishes where style is concerned; certain bookbags may be "in" at school, while others are definitely "out." An unpopular bookbag stands an excellent chance of "disappearing." (Also check to see if your child's school has any restrictions where bookbags are concerned.)

Notebooks

Children should have notebooks that make it easy to get organized and stay organized. Large loose-leaf binders with subject separators, envelopes for loose papers, and pencil cases can encourage a child to keep supplies and assignments in order. It's harder to lose or forget a loose-leaf binder than a series of thin individual folders.

Again, let your child participate in the buying decision. Many children love to pick out their own notebooks and pencil cases, put things neatly where they belong, and show off their new acquisitions to their friends.

Shopping for supplies can also be an opportunity to add any "extras" to your child's home study center. Pick up a stapler, a tape dispenser, a paper punch, and a ruler; label them with your child's name and declare them "hands-off" to the rest of the family. Little touches like these mean a lot to a child.

A student planner or calendar

Many loose-leaf binders come equipped with school-year (or all-year) calendars. If your child's doesn't, consider purchasing a teacher's planning calendar (available in school and office supplies stores) for recording short-term and long-term assignments. Or buy a student planner or calendar; several companies now offer them, and they really do help. Examples:

- ▸ *Agendamate.* A colorful laminated wall chart for planning weekly goals and daily "to do's." Premier School Agendas, 2000 Kentucky Street, Bellingham, WA 98226; toll-free telephone 1-800-447-2034.

- ▸ *Student Planner.* A loose-leaf binder with multiple features including monthly calendars, class schedule sheets, monthly planning sheets, project planning forms, inspiring monthly success messages, grade tracking sheets, and study tips. Day-Timers, Inc., One Day-Timer Plaza, Allentown, PA 18195-1551; toll-free telephone 1-800-225-5005. On the Internet's World Wide Web,* go to: http://www.daytimer.com/

- ▸ *Student Success Module.* Includes a time-management training cassette, planning calendars, assignment planners for long-term projects, and student success forms. Franklin Quest, P.O. Box 31406, Salt Lake City, UT 84131; toll-free telephone 1-800-869-1776. On the WWW: http://www.franklinquest.com/

Assignment sheets

Your child's teacher may provide these. If not, feel free to make several photocopies of the sample assignment sheets on pages 154 and 155. Slip these into your child's loose-leaf binder just ahead of the calendar, then make sure they're kept up to date throughout the school year. Check often early in the year, less often as your child begins to take responsibility for this task.

HELP!

"My son's bookbag and notebook are a mess! Papers are stuffed everywhere, and he can never find a thing."

Bookbags and notebooks can become portable trash bins. Your son needs help organizing his. After the first major clean-up (done with your assistance), require that he start each evening study session with a five-minute "tidy time." Supervise, but don't do it for him. Eventually he'll form the habit and organize his materials on his own.

---

* We've listed several Web sites throughout this book. The World Wide Web is enormous and fluid; please be aware that sites come and go and URLs (Internet addresses) change, so we can't guarantee that our information will always be current and accurate. But it should give you a start in the right direction. When in doubt, use a search engine.

"My daughter forgets her homework on purpose so she won't have to do it."

Your course of action will depend on the reason your daughter is "forgetting" her homework. Here are some possible causes to consider and solutions to try:

1. She may be seeking attention. Even "negative attention"—including displeasure and scoldings—qualifies as attention. Skip the scenes and calmly let her know that you'll work with her if she brings her homework home, but you'll pay little attention to her if she doesn't. Then follow through! When she starts "remembering" her homework (which she will), give her the positive attention you promised.

2. The homework may be too difficult for her. Confer with the teacher to determine whether your daughter is capable of handling the assignments. If she isn't, try to find out why. Is she having trouble paying attention in class or grasping new concepts? Does she need extra help? Does she simply lack self-confidence? Let the teacher make suggestions about what to do, and don't hesitate to contribute suggestions of your own. *Examples:* Maybe your daughter needs to be shown that (with a minimum of help) she can do assignments she thought were too difficult. Or perhaps the teacher can give her easier assignments until she's ready to handle more difficult ones. Or maybe the assignments can be broken up into smaller, more manageable pieces.

3. Your daughter may not recognize the importance of her homework assignments. Quite often, children don't understand why homework is assigned or how doing homework (or not doing it) affects their grades. Arrange for a three-way meeting with your daughter, her teacher, and you. Ask the teacher to explain the purpose for homework in his or her class, how it is scored, and how it factors into the final grade.

4. Your daughter may be just plain lazy. It's not very flattering, but it may be true! Start by requiring your daughter to record all of her assignments on an assignment sheet. Ask the teacher to initial the sheet daily to show that an assignment has been given, and also to initial it whenever homework is handed in. Insist on seeing the sheet every evening. (You may want to tie this to a privilege or two. *Examples:* No sheet, no TV. Or no sheet, no after-school bike rides.)

Whenever your daughter neglects to bring home the materials needed to complete an assignment, give her an alternate homework assignment or an uninteresting chore to do. Or you might try a tactic that some parents have used with success: Collect her incomplete homework on Fridays and have her spend time over the weekend finishing it. When homework starts seriously interfering with play, most children see the light.

"My son *never* brings handouts home. As a result, we never know about PTA meetings or other school functions until it's too late. And if he is given a worksheet to complete at home, it never arrives and he receives a zero on the assignment. Anything handed out in class is lost forever!"

This is a common problem. (It's amazing how children can sort through the various handouts they receive in class and manage to bring home *only* those that have to do with field trips!) Encourage your son to put all handouts in his loose-leaf binder as soon as they are given out in class. Emphasize that he is *not* to stuff them in his desk or locker, the Black Holes of the grade school set.

Post a chart on the refrigerator. Whenever your son brings home a handout (whether an announcement or a worksheet), give him a star, a check mark, or a sticker. Reward him once a certain number has been reached. Or you might give your son a "special folder" just for handouts. Let him decorate it with crayons, markers, or stickers. Ask to see the folder every evening.

As a last resort, send your son's teacher several self-addressed, stamped envelopes to be used for mailing handouts home. This may seem like giving up or giving in, but there's a catch: Have your son pay for the postage out of his allowance. This is almost guaranteed to get fast results!

"My daughter keeps track of daily assignments, but not the long-term ones. We just found out that she has a big assignment due tomorrow, and there's no way she can get it done without a lot of help from us."

Don't help her. Don't take her to the library or (worse) offer to do the work yourself. After all, it's not *your* assignment. Tell her in a matter-of-fact way that she's simply going to have to accept the consequences of not getting it done. Then show her how to fill out an assignment sheet and a calendar so she'll be better prepared next time. Monitor her assignment sheets until her track record improves.

How to help your child prepare for tests

Schools don't typically teach children how to study for tests. Some children manage well regardless, but others need step-by-step guidance. Here are some suggestions you can use to help your child prepare for tests, eliminate night-before panics, and lessen test anxiety.

Before the test

1. Find out the teacher's system for scheduling tests. Some tests might be given on a regular basis (*example:* spelling tests every Friday). Others might be more irregular or incidental (*example:* social studies tests when a chapter or unit is completed). On the day the test is announced (and provided that your child tells you about it), work with your child to plan a study schedule that doesn't leave everything for the last minute.

2. Encourage your child to study "actively." Children who underline key words in the text (if this is allowed), take notes, and write outlines while reading are more likely to do well than those who merely let their eyes wander down the page.

3. Have your child invent questions that seem likely to appear on the test. Then have her try to answer the questions. This will point out areas of study that need more attention and review.

4. Teach your child the "STAR" test-taking strategy. This is particularly useful for timed tests, although it can also be applied to untimed tests.

   Survey the test to see which items can be answered quickly.

   Take time to read the directions carefully.

   Answer the questions you can answer quickly, leaving difficult items for last.

   Reread the questions and your answers, making any needed corrections.

5. Reassure your child that it's okay to leave answers blank or guess answers if she doesn't know them or can't figure them out. Some children are reluctant to go on to the next question; they get stuck midway, and their grades suffer as a result. Your child may need to practice this on untimed tests before attempting it on timed tests.

6. Make sure that your child is well-rested and fed on the morning of the test. If time allows, you may want to take her out to breakfast so she will have pleasant associations with the day.

After the test

1. Talk to your child about the test. Which parts were easy? Which parts were difficult?

2. When the graded test is handed back, work with your child to analyze any errors. Try to determine why each error was made. Was it a careless mis-

take? Was information omitted when your child was studying for the test? Did she simply forget something covered during the study session?

3. File the test and any notes or outlines made prior to the test. These can be valuable references and study tools for later cumulative tests.

For more information on helping your child prepare for tests, see pages 96–98 and 111–114.

 **HELP!**

"My daughter either doesn't study for tests, or she informs me of a test at 9 P.M. the night before—right when she's supposed to go to bed."

Teach her how to complete an assignment sheet, with descriptions of assignments (including tests) and due dates. Go over the sheet with her on a weekly basis and use it to plan study time. Use the "Before the test" guidelines on page 26 to help her form new and/or improved study habits.

"My son crams for tests the night before and does moderately well, but he forgets the material before final exams."

First, he shouldn't be cramming—he should be studying well in advance of each test. Second, it's clear that your son needs to periodically review material he has already learned. Go over past tests with him. Look back at former worksheets, papers, and reports. He needs to understand that learning is a *process*, not a series of individual units to be memorized now and discarded later.

"I help my daughter study for tests, but I never see the test grades. The only grades I ever see are on the report card every nine weeks."

Call or visit the teacher and explain how hard you're working to help your child do well in school. Say that you'd like to see the graded tests so you can monitor your daughter's performance and the effectiveness of her study sessions.

To bribe or not to bribe?

Teachers talk a lot about "behavior modification," "rewarding children for appropriate behavior," and "withholding rewards" (or imposing unpleasant consequences) for inappropriate behavior. These may sound like descriptions of the age-old practice known as bribery.

Should you bribe your child to do homework? The answer is yes—and no. We all respond to bribery. Few adults would show up at work if they weren't paid to do so. Most of us trust that certain actions will lead to expected rewards, whether *personal* (feeling good about ourselves), *social* (being thanked or praised by others), or *material* (receiving a concrete reward). Similarly, we realize that other actions will lead to less pleasant personal, social, or material consequences.

Children's actions should also lead to consequences that are clearly spelled out ahead of time. When you set consequences, make sure that *you* can live with them! In setting consequences, what you're really doing is giving your child a choice. If your child chooses the consequence for *not* doing homework, then you must impose it with no anger, pleading, or hesitation on your part.

Most children aren't mature enough to value personal rewards, so they need more tangible external motivation. It's preferable that this take the form of social rather than material rewards (or unpleasant consequences). But if the only motivation a child will respond to is material, then you shouldn't hesitate to use this option. Just remember to gradually phase it out when it's no longer needed.

Children who are hard to motivate require frequent rewards. For this to have the desired effect, it's important that the rewards be *consistent* and appropriate to what you want the child to do. (Of course, any punishments should meet these same criteria.) Buying your child an expensive toy for completing an assignment is *not* an appropriate reward. Grounding your child for a month for failing to complete an assignment is *not* an appropriate punishment.

We recommend small rewards for achieving short-term goals, and equally small punishments for not achieving them. (*Examples:* You might award a colorful sticker or a quarter for doing an assignment, or withhold a privilege for not doing it.) Wait until later to set equivalent rewards and punishments for achieving (or not achieving) long-term goals. Once you decide on a system of rewards and consequences, you may want to use a contract to formalize the arrangement. Consider letting your child design the contract.

H E L P !

"My son finds any number of excuses to leave his homework and do something else. As a result, it often takes him all evening to complete an assignment that should take half an hour. I have lectured him, and

I have praised him when he's been at least moderately attentive. But neither of these approaches seem to work."

Try providing him with concrete rewards for completing his homework within
a reasonable amount of time. (*Example:* If he enjoys inline skating, you can
use this as a reward.) Since you don't want to give him an excuse to fail,
make your initial requirements fairly easy to satisfy. Let him skate for half an
hour after finishing half of his homework. Later in the evening, when the
other half is done, allow him extended skating time.

**"My daughter does her homework, but only when I scold her. How can
I eliminate the need for constant scolding?"**

You can decide to *stop* scolding—effective immediately. And you can end an
ongoing power struggle that isn't very satisfying for you or your daughter. You
may think that when you scold your daughter and she does her homework,
you're the winner of the power struggle. In fact, you're the loser. Your daughter has figured out precisely how much "pushing" it takes to send you over the
edge into anger. When you react to her pushing by scolding, you are actually
letting her control the situation!

Remember that *you're the adult*—you're supposed to be smarter and stronger
than she is. You can choose to ignore her pushing and focus calmly on the
task at hand. Figure out a reward that would mean something to her, and use
it to provoke the response you want to see. *Example:* If your daughter enjoys
going to the movies on the weekends, tell her she can—as long as she does her
homework. Allow some room for failure until the new pattern has been estab-
lished. Let her know that if she completes three out of four days of homework
assignments, you'll give her the money for a movie ticket. Eventually you can
increase that to four days out of four.

If you disagree with a teacher
about homework. . .

Perhaps you feel that your child is being assigned too much homework or too
little, or homework that's too hard or too easy, or homework that takes too
much time or not enough to complete. Whenever you're dissatisfied with or
uncertain about any aspect of your child's education, these are the steps to take:

1. Make an appointment to talk with your child's teacher.
2. Prepare for your conference by making a list of your questions or concerns.
   Write them down.

3. Present your questions or concerns to the teacher, then *listen to what the teacher says* in response. Don't hesitate to ask for explanations of any terms or language you don't understand.

4. If you're still dissatisfied when the conference is over, go home and think about it. (This also gives the teacher time to think about the problem and come up with solutions or strategies that may not have occurred to him during your meeting.)

5. If the problem persists, make an appointment to confer with the school principal. Follow the same procedure recommended for the teacher conference: Make a list of points you want to cover, then present them at the conference.

For most problems, there is no need to go any further than this in the school hierarchy. For the rare circumstance that does require intervention at a higher level, consult your local Board of Education representative.

We can't overemphasize the importance of starting with your child's teacher. This is the person who knows your child best and spends the most time with your child. While it may be tempting to go straight to the principal, you should always give the teacher the first chance to respond.

When and how to hire a tutor

If your child is having difficulty doing homework or other schoolwork, and if for whatever reason you are unable to provide sufficient help yourself, you should consider seeking professional help in the form of a tutor. Here are some circumstances that might lead you to take this step:

▸ Your child's teacher or the school counselor recommends it.

▸ Homework sessions with your child are frequently unpleasant or stressful.

▸ The rest of your family is suffering because of excessive time spent with one child's homework. (A second child who wants more attention can develop learning problems as a way to get it.)

▸ Your job hours vary and you're unable to set up a consistent schedule for your child's homework.

▸ Your child's school problems are severe enough to warrant outside assistance.

If the problem appears to be one of attitude rather than ability, you may want to see a counselor first. But if the causes seem to be academic *and* attitude-related, it's time to look for a tutor. Your child's school system may provide free tutorial services. Start by exploring this option. Otherwise, school administrators may be able to recommend tutors known to them or suggested by other parents or teachers.

If you decide to hire a tutor, begin with an in-person interview. Don't make your choice solely on the basis of a telephone conversation. Make sure that you both understand and agree to the following terms and expectations:

1. If the tutoring will take place in your home, you'll resist the urge to "pitch in." You can talk to the tutor briefly before each session begins and after it's over, but stay away while it's going on.

2. You'll be considerate of the tutor's time. If an after-session conference runs half an hour or longer, you'll offer to pay the tutor accordingly.

3. You'll make every effort to provide an environment free of distractions—including bouncy dogs, overheard telephone conversations, curious siblings, and other interruptions.

4. If the tutoring will take place outside your home, you'll have your child at the appointed place regularly and on time. In case of a necessary cancellation, you'll inform the tutor ahead of time.

5. The tutor and you will agree upon (and put in writing) specific goals to be worked toward with your child. Progress toward these goals will be the primary criterion you'll use in determining whether the tutor's services are satisfactory—and whether you'll continue using and paying for them.

Before the tutor starts working with your child, set up a meeting between you, the tutor, and your child's teacher. This will help the tutor to become oriented to the teacher's routines and expectations. Afterward, the tutor should keep in touch with the teacher.

Once the tutoring begins, don't expect miracles overnight. In fact, you should be suspicious of tutors who promise such miracles. Too often, parents who hire tutors in April are disappointed when their children are held back a grade in June. Some children may require tutoring for extended periods of time.

Finally, tutoring should not cause further anxiety. It's normal for a child to be somewhat anxious during the first session. But if anxiety persists after the first few sessions, stop the tutoring. Look for another tutor and try again, or schedule a teacher conference to explore other options.

Many parents today are turning to commercial learning centers or chains for tutoring help. These are often well-advertised and promise amazing success. If you're considering this option, proceed with caution. Make certain that:

▸ your child will receive individualized instruction

▸ the instruction will be based on your child's specific learning needs

▸ the center is willing to communicate and coordinate with your child's teacher

▸ you will receive regular updates about your child's progress, and

▸ the personnel at the center are highly qualified in terms of teaching credentials and years of experience.

What to do when all else fails

Some children absolutely refuse to do their homework despite rewards, consequences, promises, or threats, and despite the best and most caring efforts of parents, teachers, tutors, and other concerned persons. If your child's problems resist any and all of the troubleshooting strategies outlined in this chapter, you probably need professional assistance. Ask the teacher about the school's procedures for a psychological evaluation, or seek outside testing. Discuss the results in a conference with the teacher, the school counselor, and the principal.

A change in classroom assignment may be called for. Some children thrive when they are moved to another room at the same grade level; others need more specialized help in the form of a class for learning differences or disabilities. Or the test results may show that a child is being underchallenged and would benefit from a program for gifted students. Or they may indicate the need for a period of psychological counseling.

Try to be objective when studying the alternatives presented to you. Keep in mind your primary purpose: helping your child. With that as your goal, you're certain to make the right decision.

How to Help Your Child with Reading

"Whoever forms a reading habit will never lose it.
It is a treasure no one can take from him.
It contains wealth that neither poverty, nor old age,
nor misery can tarnish. Thieves cannot steal it
nor storms destroy it and, like vintage wine,
it can only improve with age."

Arthur Langlie

Whatever happened to Dick and Jane?

Think about your first grade class. Do you remember what reading instruction was like? If your experience was like millions of other students in the United States, you probably were placed in a reading group. When your reading group met with the teacher, you took turns reading from a basal reader (reading textbook). You might have even read books from the "Dick and Jane" series published by Scott, Foresman, the most frequently mentioned example of a basal reading series. Your teacher would help you with words you needed to learn and would ask you comprehension questions to see if you understood the story. While your teacher met with other reading groups, you might have been assigned seat work to do—frequently filling out workbook pages.

Well, guess what? Reading isn't "Dick and Jane" anymore! Some schools in the United States still use basal reading series. However, as you might imagine, the characters in basal readers today are more representative of the cultural diversity of our country. Most reading series now include classroom activities that emphasize reading/writing connections and are far more stimulating than simply filling out workbook pages. Other schools have eliminated the use of basal readers altogether and use children's books (yes, regular library books) instead.

The traditional reading groups so popular in the 1950s, '60s, '70s, and '80s are not as prevalent as they were in the past. Instead of being assigned to a particular group for an entire year or semester, your child might have whole-class instruction with children of all achievement levels mixed together. Your child's teacher might also use flexible grouping—student pairs, interest groups, literature groups, or friendship groups, depending on what is being taught and learned.

In short, reading instruction across the country varies from district to district, school to school, and class to class. As a parent, you'll want to find out how your child is being taught to read and how you can best support your child's reading efforts at home. Here are some questions to ask the teacher:

▶ "Is a reading textbook used? What grade level books are used? Are other reading materials used in the classroom in addition to or instead of a reading textbook?"

▶ "How are students grouped for reading instruction? How are grouping decisions made?"

▶ "How is word recognition taught?"

▶ "How is reading comprehension taught?"

▶ "How is my child's progress in reading monitored?"

▶ "How will I be informed if my child is falling behind in reading?"

▶ "How can I support the reading program by helping at home?"

Research has not identified one "best" or "right" way to teach reading to all students. Good teachers can teach students to read by using almost any method. What's most important is to keep track of when your child is not catching on and to respond quickly. As a parent, you must take responsibility for finding out how your child is being taught and how she is progressing. If your child is not doing well, talk to the teacher and quickly develop a plan for improving the situation.

Even though reading programs vary considerably, there are some ways to help your child that complement any reading program. In this chapter, you'll learn how to read aloud to your child, help your child read aloud, and help your child learn phonics, word patterns, sight words, and longer words, as well as how to improve reading comprehension and follow written directions.

 **HELP!**

"My daughter is in fourth grade and a terrific reader. The problem is that everyone in her class—including high, medium, and low readers—all read the same novels. Frankly, I think that my daughter is being held back. The books they read are just too simple for her, and she gets bored. On the other hand, some parents I've talked to think that their children are frustrated because the novels are too hard for them. Why don't they have reading groups like when I was in school?"

There are advantages to having students of different reading levels use the same materials and learn to read in mixed-abilities groups. Classroom discussions can be more lively, lower readers can learn from higher readers (and vice versa), and teachers can provide instruction in skills to the class as a whole. You may want to ask your daughter's teacher to provide you with lists of supplementary readings—books and other materials that are related to what the class is reading but offer more challenge in terms of reading level.

"My son is in third grade. His teacher says that she teaches reading using 'whole language.' What does that mean?"

Whole language is a philosophy of teaching that integrates reading, writing, listening, and speaking while emphasizing learning opportunities that are meaningful to children and are connected to the kinds of literacy activities they will use in real life. Different school systems, schools, and classroom teachers define whole language differently and translate the philosophy into practice in a variety of ways. Ask your child's teacher precisely what he or she means by whole language. Also ask the questions listed on page 34 to find out more about your son's reading program.

How to raise your child's reading level

First, you should know that there are three sure ways *not* to raise your child's reading level:

1. Make reading a chore that must be done for a certain amount of time every day, no matter what.
2. Tie your opinion of your child to his or her reading ability—and communicate that through your attitudes and behaviors.
3. Constantly push your child to read at a higher level.

And there's one sure way to raise your child's reading level—even if that isn't your primary goal:

Make reading fun.

If your child grows up loving to read, and that love of reading is at least partly due to your efforts, then you've given your child a gift that will last a lifetime. How can you accomplish this? By keeping this crucial fact in mind at all times: *Reading readiness occurs at different ages, just like the readiness to walk or talk.* Typically, boys are ready later than girls, although this is not always the case. Pushing a child who is not ready can cause irreparable damage by leading to negative attitudes toward reading and a negative self-image. In some European countries, children are taught to read at age seven. By then, most are ready, and they experience far less difficulty than many American children. This late start in no way impedes their long-term reading achievement.

Of course, this is not to say that children who are ready to read at an earlier age should be prevented from doing so. Some children can sight read words by age three; some can read and comprehend entire books by the time they start kindergarten. If your child is a "born reader," you probably already know this, and you've probably been feeding that eager young mind since you first became aware of its existence.

There is no "magical" point at which every child is ready to read, but there are several factors which indicate readiness:

- ▶ the ability to listen and sit still
- ▶ an interest in books and in what words say
- ▶ good vocabulary and language development
- ▶ knowledge of the alphabet, and
- ▶ the ability to discriminate between different letters and sounds.

Good "first books" include picture books, rhymes, and predictable books, all of which children enjoy. (*Examples*: "Old MacDonald Had a Farm" and some of the simpler Bill Martin and Dr. Seuss books.) When in doubt about where to start, ask a children's librarian.

If your child has progressed beyond the beginning reader's stage, your best next step is to ease further progress. Frequent trips to the library, read-aloud sessions, and parent-child conversations on a variety of topics can only heighten an interest in books that is already rooted and growing strong. The more your child reads, the better your child will read, and you will have helped to raise his reading level by doing the same things you've been doing all along.

During her term as chairperson of the International Reading Association's Parents and Reading Committee, Carole L. Riggs compiled a list of "ABC's" for caring parents. You should find these helpful today and into the future.*

The ABC's of How to Help Your Child

ACCEPT your child unconditionally.

BELIEVE in your child. Trust in his or her ability.

COMMUNICATE with your child. Share ideas.

DISCUSS things with your child.

ENJOY your child. When parents enjoy their children, children enjoy their parents.

FIND things of interest to do together.

GIVE your child responsibility that can be handled. This can lead to a feeling of accomplishment.

HELP your child with words of encouragement.

IMPRESS upon your child the vision of what is all around. Talk about the things you see, hear, taste, feel and smell.

JOIN your child in fun activities.

KEEP from over-identifying with your child. Don't try to live your life again through your child.

LISTEN to your child. He or she needs someone to share thoughts and ideas.

MODEL behavior you want to see in your child.

NAME things for your child. Labels are important.

OBSERVE the way your child goes about tasks. Provide help when needed.

PACE your child. Help your child to do one thing at a time and do it well.

QUESTION your child using question words such as "who," "what," "where," and "when." Ask about stories or everyday things that happen.

READ to your child every day.

SPEND time with your child.

TAKE your child to the library on a regular basis.

UNDERSTAND that learning isn't always easy. Sometimes we all fail. We can learn from our mistakes.

---

* Reprinted with permission of Carole L. Riggs, Ed.D. "The ABC's of How to Help Your Child." Parent Involvement Packet. Springfield, VA: Personal Press, 1983.

Value your child's school and teachers. Your attitude will often be mirrored in your child.

Write with your child. Encourage the youngster to write; even scribbles are important.

X is often an unknown quantity. What else would you like to add to this list?

You are your child's most important teacher.

Zip it all up with love. Love gives zest to life.

We'd like to add a few "X-tras" of our own to this list:

> Remember that reading *in itself* is not fun. Reading is fun only if you are interested in what you are reading.

> Set aside a time and a place for reading. Allowing children to read past bedtime is one strategy that works well.

> Visit bookstores. If you haven't noticed, bookstores are becoming "the place to be." You'll find them on Main Street, along the town square, and in shopping malls of all sizes. Book reviews, visiting authors, book clubs, and other special events are scheduled on a regular basis. Some families we know visit their favorite bookstore once or twice a month as a family outing.

> Don't be limited to books. Reading material is all around us: on cereal boxes, advertisements, signs, recipes, even the backs of buses.

> Provide your child with a book club membership or magazine subscription of his own. For magazine suggestions, see the list on pages 39–40.

> Become familiar with children's books. They seem to be getting better year after year, and they're wonderfully entertaining to read! (Have you noticed how many celebrities are writing children's books? Jimmy Buffet, Robin Williams, and Whoopi Goldberg are among a few recent examples.) Browse through the children's section of your local library or bookstore and take the time to read some children's books. You're in for a pleasant surprise.

And finally:

> Be a reader yourself. If your child never sees you read, he may conclude that reading is something that is only done in school. If a boy never has a male role model of a teacher, he may conclude that reading is only done by women. When your child asks you what you would like for a birthday or holiday gift, ask for a book—preferably one written by your child.

Recommended Magazines for Children

Boys' Life. Boy Scouts of America, 1325 Walnut Hill Lane, Irving, TX 75038-3096. Ages 8–17. "The Magazine for All Boys," published for over 85 years, features sports, hobbies, adventure stories, fun and games. Write to Boy Scouts of America or contact your local BSA council for subscription information. On the WWW: http://www.bsa.scouting.org/mags/magazine.htm

Cricket. Cricket Magazine Group, 112 Tenth Street, Des Moines, IA 50309; toll-free telephone 1-800-827-0227. Ages 9 & up. Fairy stories, folk tales, fantasy and science fiction, history, biographies, science, sports, travel, poems, rhymes, animal stories, fun, and humor for young readers. Also available from the Cricket Magazine Group: *Spider,* for beginning readers and independent young learners, liberally illustrated (ages 6–9); *Ladybug* (ages 2–6); *Muse,* sponsored by *Smithsonian,* featuring the Smithsonian's collections and research in articles, photo essays, narratives, biographies, excerpts from letters and diaries, and more (ages 6–14). On the WWW: http://www.bn1-2.com/cricket/bug4.htm

Highlights for Children. P.O. Box 182167, Columbus, OH 43218-2167; toll-free telephone 1-800-848-8922. Ages 5–12. Espousing a philosophy of "fun with a purpose," America's largest-circulation children's magazine is a venerable institution; it celebrated its 50th anniversary in 1996. It is not on the World Wide Web but is available on America Online in the Kids Only Channel.

National Geographic World. National Geographic Society, P.O. Box 2330, Washington, DC 20013-2330; toll-free telephone 1-800-647-5463. Ages 8–14. Geography, history, and more made exciting for young readers. For sample features from current issues and information on how kids can become "junior members," visit the Web site: http://www.nationalgeographic.com/ngs/mags/world/worldmag/worldmag.htm

Ranger Rick. 8925 Leesburg Pike, Vienna, VA 22184-0001; telephone (703) 790-4000. Ages 6–12. This magazine from the National Wildlife Federation features animal photos, drawings, riddles, crafts, games, and stories that turn kids on to nature, outdoor adventure, and helping the environment. On the WWW: http://www.nwf.org./nwf/lib/rr/index.html

Sports Illustrated for Kids. Time, Inc. Magazine Co., P.O. Box 830609, Birmingham, AL 35283-0609; toll-free telephone 1-800-334-2229. Ages 8 and up. Sports stories, biographies, features, and photos especially for young readers. On the WWW: go to http://pathfinder.com/ and click on Kidstuff, then click on Sports Illustrated for Kids.

Zillions—Consumer Reports for Kids. P.O. Box 1777, Boulder, CO 80323-1777; telephone (515) 237-4903. Ages 7–12. Articles, reports, and product comparisons help children and young adolescents become savvy consumers.

For a comprehensive listing, with descriptions, of magazines for youngsters, consult this excellent resource:

Magazines for Kids and Teens: A Resource for Parents, Teachers, Librarians, and Kids! edited by D.R. Stoll (Newark, DE: International Reading Association, 1994). Write to: International Reading Association, 800 Barksdale Road, P.O. Box 8139, Newark, DE 19714-8139, or call toll-free 1-800-336-READ (1-800-336-7323).

For more magazine suggestions, see pages 75–76.

How to read aloud to your child

Reading aloud to your child is the *best* way to help your child learn to read. Start early (from your child's infancy), keep going (well after your child learns how to read), and do it often (daily if possible). The importance of reading aloud to children in terms of their vocabulary acquisition, attitude toward reading, and reading ability cannot be exaggerated. When you read aloud to your child, you:

- ▶ model fluent reading
- ▶ promote enjoyment and appreciation of children's literature
- ▶ develop knowledge of new vocabulary and concepts
- ▶ stimulate and motivate independent reading, and
- ▶ develop a bond between you and your child.

There are many excellent children's books available in your school or local library. If you need help choosing, ask the librarian, who will be glad to make recommendations and point you toward children's favorites. As you search for children's literature to share with your child, let her participate actively in this process. Get your child a library card (if you haven't already). Allow her to select at least some of the books you'll be bringing home.

How can you make the most of reading aloud to your child? Here are some suggestions to try before, during, and after:

Before reading aloud

- ▶ Choose a book you enjoy.
- ▶ Choose stories with great characters and good dialogue.
- ▶ Relax.
- ▶ Set an atmosphere for enjoyment. Find a comfortable chair big enough for two, curl up together on the sofa, or arrange fat pillows on the floor. Make sure that the lighting is adequate for reading and looking at pictures.
- ▶ Read the title of the book aloud.
- ▶ Read the names of the author and illustrator.
- ▶ Look at the cover and skim through the book quickly with your child.
- ▶ Start with questions about the subject of the book, your child's experience with that subject, and predictions of what the story might be about.

While reading aloud

- ▶ Read slowly, but don't "talk down" to your child.
- ▶ Create a mood by changing the volume and pitch of your voice.
- ▶ Act out parts of the story using puppets or props.
- ▶ For younger children, make rhyming books a regular part of your reading sessions. Turn rhymes into games by reading the beginning of each line and letting your child guess the last word.
- ▶ Use your sense of humor—laugh a lot!
- ▶ Encourage discussion and questions. Allow your child to interrupt you at any point along the way.
- ▶ Share personal thoughts with each other about the pictures and story.
- ▶ Offer additional information and explain key concepts and vocabulary when your child asks or when you think it is appropriate.

After reading aloud

- ▶ Ask your child questions about the story.
- ▶ Encourage your child to ask you questions about the story. Model how to respond to questions.

▸ Let your child retell the story in her own words.

▸ Relate the story to real-life experiences.

▸ Share personal reactions with each other about likes and dislikes of the story and whether or not you would like to read another book by the same author.

10 ways to help your child read aloud

Both oral reading (reading aloud) and silent reading (reading to oneself) are important for children of any age. Schools tend to emphasize oral reading in the early grades; this helps young children concentrate and helps teachers diagnose reading difficulties. Silent reading is faster and allows children to skim, reread, or adjust their speed as necessary. Because of these factors, and because adults do far more silent reading than oral reading, the emphasis shifts as children progress through the grades.

Young children may mumble to themselves as they read "silently." As long as they need this crutch, they should not be forced to stop using it. Even adults revert back to it when they are tired, or when they are reading something that requires a lot of concentration. If it becomes a bad habit for your child, the teacher can work on gradually reducing it (and you can help at home).

Naturally, you'll want to make sure to choose books that your child can actually *read*—in other words, books that aren't too difficult or advanced. A good test of suitability is to have your child read the first page silently, raising a finger each time he comes across an unknown word. If there are more than five unknown words on the first page, try to find another, simpler book on a similar topic.

You may be surprised to discover that your child can handle material which would otherwise be out of his reach—*if* the material is something of keen interest to your child, or *if* the topic is one he already knows a lot about. The more you converse with your child, the more topics he will be familiar with. The moral of this story is: You can help your child's reading immeasurably by talking to him often and at length. As a bonus, you'll also be helping to develop your child's vocabulary and fund of general information.

It's important for your child to *understand* what he is reading. Stopping too often to decode unknown words can result in the story's meaning being lost. To minimize this problem, try these strategies:

1. Scan the story to find words that may be difficult for your child to read or understand. Go over these words with him in advance.

2. Allow your child to read through a story silently before reading it aloud. (This is particularly important for children who are self-conscious about oral reading.)

3. Read a story aloud to your child before asking him to read it. (Don't be surprised if he wants to hear the same story over and over again.) This will free him from having to decode unknown words, will clarify the story structure, and *will make reading more enjoyable*—a very important benefit. Granted, this strategy may result in more memorizing than reading, but it definitely has its place. As one child told us, "Reading can sure be fun when you know how!"

4. Let your child read a favorite story into an audiocassette recorder (preferably when there is no one around to listen). You might want to work with him to make a "greatest hits" cassette to give to grandparents, other family members, or friends. Take an old plastic cassette case and let him create a new cover with artwork or a personal photograph.

5. Have your child take turns reading parts of a story with someone else—another family member, a friend, a neighbor, a sitter, even a teddy bear.

6. Read story beginnings aloud to your child to "hook" his interest, then let your child finish the story independently.

7. Make videotapes of your child reading aloud. These become great keepsakes and also give you a way to watch your child's progress in reading over the years.

8. Add variety to reading sessions by taking turns: you read one line, he reads the next line, and so on through a story.

9. If a story includes dialogue, assume the role(s) of one or more characters and have your child take on another. Read "in character" using different voices, accents, and inflections.

10. Keep interruptions to a minimum. Save phonics lessons for later so your child won't lose track of the story line or meaning. If he misreads several words, correct only those that affect the meaning of the story. (Example: It's more important to correct *can't* read as *can* than *the* read as *a*.) Make less critical corrections at a time when he misreads only a few words and comprehends well.

How to help your child with phonics

"Phonics" refers to a way of teaching reading that emphasizes the sounds of letters and how those letter sounds blend to make words. As you have probably read and heard, phonics instruction is very controversial. Some folks insist that it's the key to learning how to read, while others contend that isolating letter sounds is unnatural.

Few would argue that letters represent sounds and that we have to know how the letters and sounds relate in order to read words. The real debate over phonics revolves around *how* phonics should be taught, not *whether* it should be taught. Should phonics be taught systematically, using carefully sequenced workbook pages? Or should phonics be taught more naturally, using children's literature and words in their everyday environment? In either case, should phonics instruction occur through varied activities, such as singing or using materials that enable children to touch and feel the letters? The controversy has been raging for decades.

What can you do? Learn how phonics will be taught in your child's school and ask how you can help at home. You can start by familiarizing yourself with the names teachers give to the basic vowel sounds.

long **a**—as in **name**   short **a**—as in **pan**

long **e**—as in **Pete**   short **e**—as in **met**

long **i**—as in **ice**   short **i**—as in **pin**

long **o**—as in **oak**   short **o**—as in **lock**

long **u**—as in **flute** or **use**   short **u**—as in **cub**

C A U T I O N

You may have seen and heard enticing TV and radio advertisements for commercial phonics programs that promise quick results. We have several concerns about such programs:

▶ Figuring out words is a process that uses three cueing systems: *phonics, meaning* cues, and *grammar* cues. Some children overuse one or more of the cueing systems and underuse the other(s). (*Example:* In the sentence, "I bought a pair of boots at the shoe store," a child who reads *boats* for *boots* is paying attention to *phonics*, because she correctly reads the word's beginning and ending. She is also attending to *grammar*, because a plural noun is what the sentence requires. However, she is not attending to *meaning*, because you can't buy boats at a shoe store.) The emphasis a particular child needs to work on can be determined through careful diagnosis. Remember that there is no single "right" way to help every child read.

▶ The pacing in a commercial program may be very rapid and may confuse children who have reading difficulties.

▶ The method and sequence of the program may not match the instruction in your child's classroom.

▶ There is a danger that busy parents might believe that paying the high cost of a phonics program can substitute for more comprehensive and essential strategies, such as reading to their children every day.

HELP!

"My daughter's teacher uses a whole language method to teach reading, but I've heard that whole language is the opposite of phonics instruction. Should I be worried that my daughter won't learn phonics?"

One myth about whole language is that it involves no phonics instruction. In general, the idea behind whole language is that phonics isn't taught through dry, boring workbooks; rather, the sounds of the language (and how they are represented in print) are taught through engaging reading, writing, listening, and speaking activities. In other words, the sounds of the language are taught naturally, using materials that are entertaining to students. Still, you might ask the teacher how phonics is being taught, and more specifically, how your child is progressing in learning the sounds of the language and relating those sounds to reading the printed word.

"My son sounds out almost every word on the page and has no idea what he is reading. What can I do?"

Your son may have been taught to read with an excessive dose of phonics. He needs to learn that this approach doesn't always work. You may want to let him record his reading on audiocassette. By reading and rereading passages into the tape recorder and listening to his tapes, he may develop greater fluency. You may also want to use flash cards with words he misses frequently to help him develop a large bank of sight words. Most importantly, emphasize to your son the importance of reading for meaning.

"My daughter reverses letters when she reads. I'm afraid she might be dyslexic."

Just as Mommy is Mommy whether viewed from the front or the back, some young children see *b* as *b* even when it's facing the other way. If such reversals persist into the third grade, talk to the teacher. Rather than immediately suspecting the presence of dyslexia—a nebulous term used differently by different professionals—try the solutions presented on page 65.

How to help your child with word patterns

Even very young readers are good at detecting word patterns. In fact, they are usually much better at detecting word patterns than they are at learning phonics or spelling rules. Fortunately, knowledge of word patterns is an important reading skill. For example, if your child can read the word *pet*, then you can help her discover that *met* and *set* follow the same pattern. Similarly, recognizing *pet* can lead to an understanding of how to read *pen* and *peg*.

You can help your child learn basic word patterns. Did you know that 500 words can be built from the following 37 fragments? Use these patterns to make lists of rhyming words with your child. (*Examples:* back, pack, sack; bail, fail, hail, jail, mail, pail, rail, sail, tail; gain, main, pain, rain.) Your child will have more fun and learn more quickly if you use individual letters made of plastic or printed on small cards that she can move around. Start with two-letter patterns and gradually add others to her repertoire.

-ack	-at	-ide	-ock
-ail	-ate	-ight	-oke
-ain	-aw	-ill	-op
-ake	-ay	-in	-ore
-ale	-eat	-ine	-ot
-ame	-ell	-ing	-uck
-an	-est	-ink	-ug
-ank	-ice	-ip	-ump
-ap	-ick	-it	-unk
-ash			

C A U T I O N

Be careful about telling your child to "look for the little words inside the big words." This can lead to words like *prepare* turning into *prep* and *are*.

How to help your child with sight words

All children need to develop a set of words that they can recognize instantly. Some English words are best learned by sight, as they have no sound-symbol regularity; common examples are *there* and *one*. Other words occur so frequently in the English language that they should be known immediately; it's simply not efficient to sound them out.

You can help your child develop a bank of words that he can recognize quickly and easily. Ask the teacher to supply you with a list of words for your child to learn by sight. This list may be derived from your child's basal reader, or it may be recommended by your school system. If the teacher can't give you a list, you may want to use one of the sample lists found on pages 156–161. Compiled by Edward Fry, these lists of words that occur frequently in children's books are well respected and widely used.

Here's how to get started with sight words training:

1. Choose three words for your child to learn.
2. Write the first word on an index card.
3. Pronounce the word.
4. Talk about what the word means.
5. Work together to think of a sentence using the word. Write the sentence on the back of the index card.
6. Repeat steps 2–5 for the other two words.
7. At the end of the session, review all three words.
8. The next time you meet, flash the three words to your child. For each one he reads correctly, put a check mark on the index card. If he misses a word, offer encouragement, show him the sentence on the back of the card, and review the pronunciation and meaning of the word.
9. Add a few new words.
10. After a word gets five checks, enter the word into your child's personal dictionary (a notebook with one alphabet letter per page). Review the words in the dictionary from time to time.

How many words should you attempt to teach during a single session? That depends on your child's age, attention span, and tolerance for frustration, as well as the level of difficulty of the words you're teaching. We recommend that you start with three words per session and increase this number gradually as time permits (and your child's interest allows). Build up to a maximum of 15–20 minutes of study per day for primary students, 30 minutes per day for older students.

Most of us have forgotten enormous amounts of information we learned as children. Information not used quickly "disappears" from our memories. That's why it's important to review anything you teach your child. Different children will, of course, require different amounts of review. We suggest these general guidelines:

▶ For children of above-average ability, it may take 15–20 exposures to a new word before it becomes a part of their long-term vocabulary.

▶ For children of average or below-average ability, this may take 35–65 meaningful exposures.

Be patient—and remember that what you're doing is important to your child's reading success, which directly affects your child's school success *and* life success.

Using games to practice sight words and word patterns

Before too long, both you and your child will grow weary of using flash cards and lists to practice reading skills. Homemade games can add variety, spark, and enjoyment to what's basically a rote task. Here are four suggestions you can try:

1. Make Bingo, Tic-Tac-Toe, Dominoes, or board games targeting specific words. (These can be fun family projects.) For suggestions, see Chapter 9.

2. Make a double set of flash cards and play Concentration (see pages 141–142), a game in which it's easy to add new words or replace learned words. Words read correctly can be fed into a piggy bank.

3. Invent riddles. *Example*: "I'm thinking of a word that starts like *pet* and rhymes with *man*."

4. Adapt almost any card game for instructional purposes. Instead of matching numbers or suits, children can match words that rhyme (*hat, that*), words that have the same vowel sound (*bake, aim*), or words that have

the same blend (*slow*, *sly*) or digraph (*child*, *chore*), to name just a few. (A digraph is a group of two successive vowels—*oi*, *oy*, *ow*, *ou*—or consonants—*sh*, *ch*, *th*, *wh*—that form a single sound.)

How to help your child with longer words

By the end of the primary school years, most children are reading multisyllabic words. If they are to become rapid readers, they must learn to recognize frequently occurring prefixes, suffixes, and roots. This is the way most adults tackle unknown words. *Example:* An adult reading *microorganism* might recognize the prefix *micro-* as meaning "very small," the root *-organ-* as meaning "alive," and the suffix *-ism* as indicating that the word is a noun.

For fun, test your own facility on the longest word in the English language (and you thought it was *antidisestablishmentarianism*):

pneumoultramicroscopicsilicovolcanoconiosis

Try to decipher this *before* checking an unabridged dictionary!

When teaching your child prefixes and suffixes, work on only a few at a time. Since it's easier to teach prefixes than suffixes (their meanings are more concrete), focus on prefixes first.

▸ The most effective approach is to teach each prefix in the context of several words. *Example:* Teach *dis-* in *disagree*, *disappear*, and *disobey*.

▸ Be sure that the words you choose are good examples of the prefix. *Example:* For teaching *in-* as the opposite of *out-*, *inside* is a good example while *incorrect* is not.

▸ Present each new word in a sentence pair that focuses on its meaning. *Example:* "I agree with you. She *disagrees* with you."

Common Prefixes

PREFIX	*MEANING*	*EXAMPLES*
bi-	two	bicycle, binoculars
dis-	not	disagree, disappear, disobey
ex-	out of	exit, expel
in-	into	inside, infiltrate
in-	not	incorrect, insincere
mis-	wrong	misspell, mistake
pre-	before	prefix, precede
post-	after	postwar, posterior

re-	again; anew	reread, rewrite
re-	back	return, retreat
sub-	under	submarine, subway
super-	above; over	superman, superior
trans-	across	transportation, transition
tri-	three	tricycle, triangle
un-	not	unhappy, untrue

When teaching your child suffixes, it's usually enough if she learns to recognize the pronunciation of the chunks (*example: -tion* = "shun") and can tell whether the suffix indicates a noun, verb, adjective, or adverb. Only suffixes with clear meanings (*examples: -ess* = woman, *-ful* = full, *-less* = without) should be taught to elementary school children, following the suggestions given above for teaching prefixes.

Common Suffixes: Nouns

SUFFIX	*EXAMPLES*
-al	removal, approval
-ance	clearance, importance
-ence	absence, presence
-ity	stupidity, curiosity
-ment	excitement, argument
-ness	fairness, craziness
-sion	division, explosion
-tion	multiplication, addition, subtraction

Common Suffixes: Nouns That Refer to Persons

SUFFIX	*EXAMPLES*
-ant	servant, giant
-ent	student, president
-er	farmer, teacher, dancer
-ess	waitress, actress
-ist	artist, cartoonist
-or	actor, sailor

Common Suffixes: Verbs

SUFFIX	*EXAMPLES*
-en	strengthen, weaken
-ify	beautify, glorify
-ize	summarize, capitalize

Common Suffixes: Adjectives

SUFFIX	*EXAMPLES*
-able	movable, drinkable
-al	musical, choral
-ent	present, absent
-ful	careful, thoughtful
-ic	artistic, gigantic
-ive	creative, active
-less	careless, thoughtless
-ly	sadly, truly
-ous	curious, religious
-y	curly, shiny, leafy

Common Suffixes: Adverbs

SUFFIX	*EXAMPLES*
-ally	naturally, totally
-ly	slowly, quickly

For lists of word patterns, prefixes, suffixes, roots, and other reading-related lists, see *The Reading Teacher's Book of Lists*, Third Edition, by E.B. Fry, J.E. Kress, and D.L. Fountoukidis (Englewood Cliffs, NJ: Prentice Hall, 1993).

How to help your child understand and respond to stories

Have you ever heard someone say, "I'm sorry I saw the movie—the book was so much better, and the characters in the movie weren't as I imagined"? When many of us read a story, we create a "movie" in our minds. We envision the setting, identify with the characters, and respond with empathy, anger, excitement, joy, sadness, or fear. The story comes alive.

How can you make stories come alive for your child? Following are some suggestions for helping your child become personally involved with a story. This engagement can not only improve your child's understanding of the story, but also spark meaningful responses to the author's message.

Sometimes it's easier to help your child understand and respond to stories when you read them aloud. However, as your child gets older, he will begin to read independently. The following suggestions can be used whether you read along with your child or he reads on his own.

1. Get ready.

Before reading, think about ways to get your child involved with the story. If the story is set in a place or time that is unfamiliar to your child, bring out the atlas or encyclopedia and help him think about where and when the story takes place.

2. Get set.

After your child has read the first few pages or chapters, talk about the main character in the story. Try to get your child "involved" with the character and his or her situation. Help your child imagine what he would do if placed in a similar situation. Help him think about how the character and the character's circumstances relate to his own life.

3. Go!

As your child reads the story, check in from time to time to see how the character's situation is developing, how your child is reacting to the developments, and what he predicts will happen next. Have him read aloud sections of the story that he thinks are particularly meaningful. You may want to give him several bookmarks or sticky notes to mark special passages to share with you.

4. Cool down.

Immediately after reading the story, talk with your child about personal reactions to the story. What did he like and dislike about it? Did the story introduce moral or ethical issues that he wants or needs to discuss with you? Also talk with your child about the author's writing style.

5. Follow up.

Often, when your child's teacher assigns a story, the assignment will also include activities for your child to complete before, during, or after reading. When this isn't the case, you might think about how your child can respond to the story through art, writing, drama, cooking, or perhaps by reading another book from the same genre or by the same author.

How to help your child understand informational text

Informational (expository) text is designed to teach—to provide information about a topic. Science, social studies, and health textbooks are examples of informational text. Informational textbooks are frequently loaded with new concepts, vocabulary, and facts. Often, students are required not only to read this information but also to learn it for tests, so quick, superficial reading won't do. Here are some suggestions for helping your child understand informational text:*

1. Preview the reading assignment. Take a look at the pictures, the headings and subheadings, the Introduction, and any summaries.

2. Talk briefly about the topic of the reading assignment. Ask your child what she already knows about the topic and what she would like to learn about it.

3. Break up the reading assignment into a few short sections (headings and subheadings should help).

4. Read the first section with your child—either silently or aloud, whatever seems most appropriate.

5. Talk about words, sentences, or ideas that seemed difficult or confusing to your child. (We like to call these areas of difficulty "clunks.")

6. Work together to think of ways to "fix up" the "clunks." (*Example:* Your child may need to look up a word in a glossary, reread a sentence, or read ahead to get a clue about the meaning of a new concept.)

7. Ask your child to tell you the key ideas from the section you read. (We call these "golden nuggets.")

8. Read the next section. Once again, talk about "clunks" and "golden nuggets."

9. After reading the whole assignment, talk about the most important ideas that your child learned. Have her predict questions that the teacher might ask on a test.

10. Think together about what else you would like to learn about the topic.

---

* Adapted from *Collaborative Strategic Reading in Heterogeneous Classrooms* by J.K. Klingner, S. Vaughn, and J.S. Schumm (1996). Manuscript submitted for publication.

This procedure takes some time, but it's worth the effort. By following these steps, your child can learn how to link new information to what she already knows, how to fix up "clunks" (areas of potential difficulty), and how to identify the most important ideas in a reading passage.

"My daughter knows what most of the words in her social studies book say, but she doesn't comprehend well."

This problem could be due to one or more of the following reasons:

- ▶ Your daughter's background of vocabulary and general information may not be adequate for comprehension of the material.

- ▶ She may be paying so much attention to saying the words "right" that she has no energy left for comprehension.

- ▶ She may not understand that the purpose of reading is comprehension, not word-calling.

- ▶ She may not know how to alter her reading speed according to her purpose for reading, and according to the demands of the material.

In any case, follow the steps described on pages 51–54 for reading stories or informational text.

In addition, you may want to encourage your daughter to visualize what she is reading. Because today's children watch so much TV, they don't form the habit of making mental pictures of their own. Try one or both of these approaches:

1. Have your daughter draw pictures to illustrate what she is reading. Eventually she will be able to describe her mental pictures to you.

2. Take every opportunity to work on oral comprehension. *Example:* After watching a TV program together, ask your daughter questions like these:

   - ▶ To relate the story to her own life: "Has anything like this ever happened to you?"

   - ▶ To help her focus: "What were the main ideas in this program?"

   - ▶ To help her recall facts from the program: "Who were the main characters?" "What did they do?" "When did the character realize that something important had happened?" "Where did this story take place?"

- To help her recognize a logical sequence: "What happened after _____ found out that _____?"
- To help her predict outcome: "What do you think will happen next?"
- To promote critical thinking: "What would have happened if _____?" "Do you agree with what happened in the story? Why or why not? Do you disagree? Why or why not?"

"My son is in the fifth grade. He reads stories at home to prepare for reading tests, but he fails them every time."

A casual reading of a story may not be sufficient preparation for a reading test in the middle grades. Meet with your son's teacher to inquire about the test format and find out what types of errors your son is making; it may be that the reading test is based on skills learned in class rather than mastery of the story content. If the test is story-based, you can help your son study for future tests by using the story study guides on pages 162–163 or 164–165.

How to help your child follow written directions

Children (and adults) often begin a task without bothering to read the directions first. You should encourage and expect your child to read directions—as long as they are at a level at which your child is capable of reading. If they aren't, model reading them for your child.

When directions are complex, follow these steps:

1. Read the entire set of directions aloud, slowly and carefully.
2. Underline or circle the action(s) to be taken (the verb or verbs).
3. If the steps are not already numbered, identify and number them.
4. Help your child to follow the directions.
5. Afterward, check to make sure that the directions were followed correctly.

All children need to know how to read and follow directions, and this is a skill that should be taught and reinforced early. A child who can't decipher and understand directions is a child who will have difficulty completing assignments and taking tests.

How to help your child with reading homework: A few final words

Learning to read is the key to all learning. Appalling numbers of American students are graduating from high school functionally illiterate, unable to read job applications or simple instructions. As a caring parent, there are few responsibilities you should take as seriously as making sure that your child learns to read.

We often travel around our state and around the country, visiting schools and talking with teachers. We have learned how tremendously reading instruction varies from place to place. With that in mind, we offer the following general advice:

1. Ask questions about your child's reading program and his or her progress in reading.

2. Ask about specific things you can do to coordinate with your child's teacher.

3. Take immediate steps to find more intensive help for your child if necessary.

Finally, as a caring parent, it's important to recognize that you are the *best* person to help your child learn to understand the purpose for reading and to enjoy reading. Your own daily reading of newspapers, magazines, recipes, directions, letters, and books will demonstrate to your child the function and importance of reading. Reading aloud to your child, listening to your child read aloud, taking trips to the library, purchasing books and magazines as gifts, and talking about favorite books and stories are all powerful ways to share the joy of reading. The best reading homework of all is the kind of real reading you do in your home.

 **HELP!**

"My son's teacher told me that he is having trouble with phonics. A friend of mine who's an elementary school teacher gave me some materials to use at home. My son did just fine on these, but his grade in reading is still a D."

Phonics can be taught and tested in many different ways. The materials supplied by your friend may address phonics or other word recognition skills in ways that your son's reading materials at school do not. Show the materials to

h   .sk to see your son's in-class work and tests, and ask your son's
t   .rnish you with supplementary materials to use at home.

in third grade. He is still having trouble with letter sounds and
y a few basic words. The teacher has referred him for testing for
rogram, but that could take months—maybe most of this school
.nwhile, he seems to be slipping farther and farther behind."

mily doesn't have the resources for private testing and tutoring, you
take positive action. Request a meeting with the school principal,
's teacher, and the special education teacher or reading specialist in
n's school. Ask specifically what you can do at home to help your son
.ading while you're waiting for his evaluation for a special program.

'aughter is in fifth grade. Even though she loved being read to when
she was little, now she refuses to read at all—she says it's 'boring.' I know
she *can* read, because her reading achievement test scores are great. She
just *won't* read."

When children proclaim, "I don't read because it's boring," quite often it's
because they haven't found the right books! Here are some suggestions for
helping your daughter find the right books:

1. Spend some time with her at the library and bookstore. Bookstores today
   are lively, active places—many seem more like community centers.

2. Make it a point to talk informally about books with your daughter. When
   she was younger, reading aloud to her was a social activity—a time for the
   two of you to bond. Now that she's older, sharing ideas about books you've
   both read, or books that you've read individually, can be a new opportunity
   for bonding.

3. Consider her interests. Does she like rock music, swimming, animals,
   sports? There are plenty of books available on all of these topics.

4. Still no "right book"? Move on to her needs. Does she want to learn how to
   redecorate her room, take photographs, or use e-mail? Would she like to
   learn more about Colorado to help plan for a family vacation? There are
   tons of books available on any and all of these subjects.

5. No "right book" yet? Talk with your daughter about her favorite movie or
   television show. Talk with the bookstore or library staff about books focus-
   ing on related genres, topics, or story lines.

6. Don't give up! The "right book" is out there. Keep looking until you find it.

How to Help Your Child with Spelling and Writing

"The art of writing is the art of applying
the seat of the pants to the seat of the chair."

Mary Heaton Vorse

What's new in spelling and writing instruction?

As you start helping your child with homework, you may find that significant changes have taken place in spelling and writing instruction since you were a child. Chances are that your instruction emphasized form over substance. As a result, many adults today don't write unless they absolutely have to, and even then they do it grudgingly. Following are descriptions of some differences you're likely to see—differences that may result in future adults who write well and actually *enjoy* writing.

A greater understanding of developmental spelling

Much has been learned about how children progress through stages of "temporary spelling," much as they progress from crawling to walking and from babbling to understandable speech. Teachers now know that a child who spells *love* "l" has made progress from spelling it "s," and they know to nudge to gradually get "lv," "luv," and eventually "love."

An emphasis on substance first

Teachers today use a writing process in which they try to get substance out first. Then and only then do they move to expecting nice handwriting and correctness in spelling and grammar. Of course, word processors greatly simplify this process! Teachers may move children from drafting to editing and polishing when there is a purpose for polishing, but not otherwise. Similarly, you will move from a draft to a final product with a letter to the editor, but not with your grocery list.

Less use of textbooks

You may find less reliance on textbooks and more instruction stemming from actual writing. Rather than having to complete the endless grammar exercises we all dreaded, your child may learn principles of grammar by viewing pieces of writing on an overhead projector and following up with writing of his own. When students learn grammar through composition, they see the purpose for their learning.

More attention to student choice

Just as you give your child some choice at home, perhaps in the toys he plays with or the color of his room, teachers recognize the value of giving children some choice in school. For example, you might find that your child is allowed to choose some of his own spelling words, which probably includes words he actually uses in his writing. Children are more likely to remember words they select than words assigned by a teacher. Other areas where you might see some choice include the types of writing students do (essays, poems, short stories, scripts) and the topics they write about.

More varied forms of assessment

When you think "assessment," you probably think "tests" and "letter grades." Teachers today use more variety in their assessment practices. For example, your spelling grade might have depended mostly or exclusively on spelling tests, which didn't necessarily help you to remember the words two weeks after the tests. In contrast, today's teachers use other means of assessment besides or in addition to tests. Your child might keep his writing in a portfolio, which you can examine to see his actual use of spelling and other skills he has learned.

When you wrote compositions, you probably got them back with letter grades and lots of red ink. Your child's teacher may correct more sparingly, and in a color other than red! Because teachers today are aware that children can't concentrate on too much at any one time, they may focus on correcting for one or two skills and save the others for a later time.

How these changes are reflected in homework

Taken together, these changes are likely to mean:

- ▶ *less* use of worksheets, *more* use of plain paper
- ▶ *less* time preparing for spelling tests, *more* spelling practice in compositions, and
- ▶ *less* homework from textbooks, *more* homework with a real-life purpose.

How to help your child with spelling

Weekly spelling tests are a time-honored tradition in American education. However, spelling programs differ from school to school and from class to class. As you prepare to help your child with spelling, start by finding out how the program in her class is organized and run. Early in the school year, take these questions to a meeting with the teacher:

About the organization of the program

- ▶ "How is the class organized for spelling? As a whole class? In spelling groups? For individualized spelling?"
- ▶ "Is the program self-paced? Can each child move through spelling lessons at his or her own rate?"

About your child's placement

- ▶ "Has my child been placed on, above, or below grade level in spelling?"
- ▶ "Is there any way for my child to have harder or easier spelling words, if necessary?"

About the program schedule

- ▶ "When are spelling words assigned or selected?"
- ▶ "When is spelling homework due?"
- ▶ "If there are spelling tests, when are they given?"

About the format of the spelling test

- ▶ "Does the test consist of words only?" Or . . .
- ▶ "Does the test include other exercises, such as sentence dictation or proofreading?"

About progress reports

- ▶ "How is spelling progress reported to parents?"
- ▶ "If report card grades are given in spelling, are they based on weekly spelling tests, on spelling assignments, and/or on other assignments, such as compositions?"

Please be aware that these questions don't have right or wrong answers. They are designed simply to help you gather information. If there's something you don't agree with or would like to see changed, talk it over with the teacher.

How to help your child study spelling words

Each child learns differently, and this includes spelling words. The "ideal" number of study sessions, the "right" length of study sessions, and the "best" way to study will not be the same for every child. Experiment with your child to determine which approach works best—and be patient; it may take a while. Here are some suggestions for getting started:

Set up a study schedule.

- ▶ On the day spelling words are assigned or selected, test your child on these words. Determine which ones she already knows and which ones she needs to study. For the latter, determine which *parts* of the words she already knows.
- ▶ Budget study time for the number of days allotted. Set aside time to practice new words and time to review previously mastered words.
- ▶ Limit spelling study sessions to 15–20 minutes each. Several shorter daily sessions are more productive than a night-before-the-test marathon cram session. Brief practices can be squeezed into spare moments: while driving to soccer, while waiting in the doctor's office, and so on.
- ▶ Plan a review of all words the night before the test.

Determine the way (or ways) your child learns best. Mix-and-match the following teaching methods:

▶ Have your child write each word 5, 10, or 15 times. (This works best if she writes *all* the words one time, then *all* the words a second time, and so on.)

▶ Have your child type words on a computer and check herself with a spellchecker program. Playing with fonts and sizes can add an extra dimension of fun!

▶ Write each word in large letters for your child. Then have her trace each one with a finger and pronounce it while tracing. Repeat until she can write the word from memory.

▶ Dictate each word to your child and have her write it down. Then have her correct the paper or slate. This encourages closer attention to mistakes.

▶ Say the words into a tape recorder. Leave enough "lag time" after each so your child can write the word. This will permit repeated practices—as many as necessary, and as many as she wants—with minimal parental involvement.

▶ New writing techniques can make spelling fun. Writing with a finger in shaving cream on a desk or back car window can have the added benefit of a clean surface once the session is over! Favorite color crayons and markers are other possibilities.

▶ Spelling can also be taught through the use of games. See Chapter 9 for suggestions.

HELP!

"My daughter's teacher lets her spell any way she wants. He calls it 'inventive spelling.' How is she ever going to learn to spell correctly?"

Your daughter's teacher probably recognizes that children go through natural developmental stages in learning to write and spell. Teachers today often encourage students to "invent" their own spellings so children can focus on meaning while writing. Making up spellings can also help students become sensitive to the relationships between letters and sounds. Most teachers who encourage students to use these temporary spellings have a well-developed instructional program to help students move through the stages of writing and spelling development. Check with your daughter's teacher to learn more about how he plans to help the children in his class move to more conventional spellings.

"My son and I work on spelling words for at least an hour every Thursday night for the test on Friday. Yet he still fails his spelling tests! Our study sessions are tiring, tension-producing, and obviously nonproductive."

The following sample schedule may help improve your son's productivity and make the study experience more enjoyable for both of you. Remember to keep study sessions short—no more than 15–20 minutes.

Sample Spelling Study Schedule

Monday

1. Pretest on the whole list, noting correct and incorrect parts of words not yet mastered.
2. Teach the first 1/3 of the words missed on the pretest.
3. Test on all words learned so far.

Tuesday

1. Test on all words learned to date.
2. Teach the second 1/3 of words missed on Monday's pretest.
3. Test on all words learned so far.

Wednesday

1. Test on all words learned to date.
2. Teach the third 1/3 of words missed on Monday's pretest.
3. Test on all words learned so far.

Thursday

1. Test on all words learned to date.
2. Practice the most difficult words.
3. Test again.

Friday

Send your child off to school with these words: "We practiced for your spelling test all week. We know you're prepared. Do the best you can today, and however you do will be fine with me."

"Every Monday, my daughter's teacher writes the week's spelling words on the board. Every Monday afternoon, my daughter comes home with a list of misspelled words to study. We never know what to study because she doesn't have a spelling book."

Meet with the teacher to determine the root of your daughter's problem. She may have difficulty copying from the board, and she may need her vision checked. Or she may be perfectly capable of copying the words but isn't taking the time to do so.

"Every week, I give my son his spelling words and he spells them out loud to me, but then he fails his weekly spelling test. How can he know the words so well and still not pass the tests?"

Practicing spelling words orally is only one way to learn them, and it may not be the best way for your son. Try some of the other strategies outlined on page 62. Make sure that your son practices *writing* the words, not just saying them.

"My daughter gets 100 percent right on every spelling test. Do I really need to help her study each week?"

It may be sufficient to pretest her on the day spelling words are assigned and let her work independently from there. If she continues to ace the tests, however, you may want to schedule a conference with the teacher to find out why. Possible reasons include:

- ▸ The spelling list words may not be challenging enough for your daughter. She may need to be moved to a higher spelling group, or be given a list of supplemental challenge words to work on.

- ▸ The words may be of an appropriate level of difficulty, but the teacher may provide enough in-class drill that practice at home is not necessary.

How to help your child with handwriting

Helping your child with handwriting takes patience, patience, and more patience. Many children simply don't like the process of writing by hand. (Many adults don't, either. Why else are typewriters and word processors so popular?) We know one young boy who will gladly spend hours making elaborate drawings of buildings, cars, airplanes, and other complicated subjects, yet the moment he's asked to write a sentence he wails, "I *can't!* It's *too hard!*" Nevertheless, all children *must* master these skills to some degree. With firm and caring assistance, even the most reluctant writer will eventually come around!

When to worry about letter reversals

Among reading professionals, a great deal of controversy exists around the topic of letter and word reversals. For example, many experts maintain that reversals are not the *cause* of learning problems but a *symptom*. They disagree among themselves about the best way to approach this issue and which remedial tactics are most effective. Naturally, this controversy has led to widespread confusion among parents.

All children who make reversals do not "have dyslexia," any more than all thin children have anorexia nervosa. Before concluding that your child has learning problems, consider the following:

▶ Reversals are quite common among children in the primary grades. They usually begin to subside by age 8 or 9.

▶ Reversals of the letters *b* and *d* can sometimes be eliminated if the child is taught this simple trick: Have the child make two fists with thumbs stuck up to form a "bed." The *b* in the word *bed* is its head (left hand); the *d* is its foot (right hand). (Since most children write on their hands anyway, go ahead and give your child permission to do it this time. The lesson will be even more unforgettable.)

▶ If the problem persists, or if the reversals are coupled with other obvious learning difficulties, consider having your child professionally evaluated. Ask the teacher about the school's procedures or seek outside testing.

How to improve your child's printing

Many children have difficulty learning to print. If this seems to be true for your child, it may be due to one or more of the following reasons:

▶ The teacher isn't allowing enough in-class practice time.

▶ Your child isn't interested in writing.

▶ Your child doesn't realize that legible writing is an important means of communication.

▶ Your child's fine motor coordination may be developing more slowly than that of other children in the class.

There are many ways to help your child improve his printing skills. Experiment with the techniques described below, or ask the teacher for additional suggestions. See page 166 for a chart showing the traditional Zaner-Bloser style of printing; you may want to copy and use this chart for practice sessions at home. *Important:* Check with the teacher first to make sure that the Zaner-Bloser style is the one your child is learning in school. If the teacher is using another style, ask for a manuscript chart you can use at home. Also make sure that your sequence or pacing of instruction does not conflict with the teacher's plan for the year.

▶ Allow 10–15 minutes per night, four nights per week for printing practice.

▶ Teach four letters per week for 13 weeks. Start with the lower-case letters, then move on to the capital letters.

Once your child has learned a few letters, use the following routine to ready him for forming words:

1. During each week's first practice session, have your child practice the first two letters of the week on manuscript practice paper. See page 167 for a sample you can copy and give to your child.

2. During each week's second practice session, have your child practice the letters in real words on manuscript practice paper. Assign words that position the new letter at the beginning, the middle, and the end. *Examples:* <u>s</u>ee, mu<u>s</u>t, pet<u>s</u>.

3. Repeat steps 1 and 2 for the remaining two letters and the next two practice sessions.

4. During each week's final practice session, have your child review all letters learned to date. For this practice, he should use regular writing paper rather than manuscript practice paper.

Keep practice sessions brief and fun. Permit the use of colored pencils, crayons, and various other writing instruments to further motivate your child.

Following each practice session, have your child examine his writing and identify ways it can be improved. The "3S" method is one way to approach this. Your child asks himself these questions about each letter:

"Is the letter the right **S**ize?"

"Is the letter the right **S**hape?"

"Did I leave enough **S**pace between letters and words?"

Encourage your child to write by posting practice pages on the refrigerator or sending them to grandparents or other admiring adults.

How to improve your child's cursive writing

Many children have difficulty making the transition from printing (manuscript) writing to cursive (script) writing. If this seems to be true for your child, it may be due to one or more of the following reasons:

- ▶ The teacher isn't allowing enough in-class learning and practice time.
- ▶ Your child may have problems writing individual letters
- ▶ Your child may be able to write the letters correctly but has problems connecting them.
- ▶ Comments from the teacher may be so general (*example:* "Your handwriting is messy") that they give no real direction for improvement.
- ▶ Your child may not like to write, and as a result may be hasty and careless with letter and word formation.

In our experience, most intermediate students can substantially improve their formation and connection of cursive letters with regular, systematic, intensive practice. And once they learn to write correctly, their speed and attitude improve.

We believe that children should be allowed to write in whichever way is most comfortable for them—printing *or* cursive—after they have learned both modes. We also believe that children should be taught to use a typewriter and/or word processor if all else fails. Following are several suggestions for helping your child master cursive. See pages 168–171 for a Zaner-Bloser cursive chart, a practice sample, and practice paper you can copy and use at home. (Again, check with the teacher first to make sure that Zaner-Bloser is the style your child is learning in school.)

We have found that practice paper is especially effective in motivating children to develop a uniform size and slant for their cursive letters. Colored magic markers (the thin-point, felt-tipped variety) make it fun and easy because they literally glide across the page.

One more tip before you begin: Cursive practice is more than an intellectual learning process; it's also a *physical* learning process. The hand, wrist, arm, elbow, and shoulder must be taught specific patterns of movement. The more your child practices, the more habitual these patterns will become. (In a way, learning to write cursive is a lot like learning to ride a bicycle.)

▸ Allow 10–15 minutes per night, four nights per week for cursive practice.

▸ Teach four letters per week for 13 weeks. Start with the lower-case letters, then move on to the capital letters.

1. During each week's first practice session, have your child practice the first two letters of the week on cursive practice paper. See page 171 for a sample you can copy and give to your child.

2. During each week's second practice session, have your child practice the letters in real words on cursive practice paper. Assign words that position the new letter at the beginning, the middle, and the end. *Examples:* <u>b</u>ook, a<u>b</u>le, so<u>b</u>.

3. Repeat steps 1 and 2 for the remaining two letters and the next two practice sessions.

4. During each week's final practice session, have your child review all letters learned to date. For this practice, she should use regular writing paper rather than cursive practice paper.

Keep practice sessions brief and fun. Permit the use of colored pencils, crayons, and various other writing instruments to further motivate your child.

Following each practice session, have your child examine her writing and identify ways it can be improved. The "4S" method is one way to approach this. Your child asks herself these questions about each letter:

"Is the letter the right **S**ize?"

"Is the letter the right **S**hape?"

"Are all the letters **S**lanted in the same direction and at the same angle?"

"Did I leave enough **S**pace between letters and words?"

Supplement practice sessions with opportunities for "real" writing. Invite your child to help you prepare party invitations, shopping lists, and thank-you notes. Encourage her to write letters to grandparents or friends.

 **HELP!**

"My daughter's handwriting is awful! When she was in the primary grades, her papers were just fine. But now that she's in third grade and has to use cursive, her teacher is constantly writing negative comments on her papers."

Talk with the teacher to discover the source of your daughter's problem. Cursive is usually introduced in the third grade, so the teacher is right on schedule. Your daughter may simply need more practice than other children in her class. Make regular practice sessions a part of her daily homework schedule.

"My son knows how to make all of his cursive letters, yet his papers are still a mess. He refuses to slow down and write neatly."

Your son needs to understand that legible writing is a form of good manners. When our writing is messy, we're implying that we don't care whether someone else can read it or not. Also, many people judge others by their written work. Tidy, readable writing makes a good first impression that lasts.

Try letting your son use a stopwatch or a kitchen timer during his practice sessions. Encourage him to work quickly but neatly. Emphasize that it's possible to write rapidly in cursive while maintaining legibility.

"My son's cursive is beautiful. The teacher admits that he can write better than she does! Is it really necessary for him to participate in cursive lessons and practices at school?"

Probably not, but talk to the teacher before expressing this opinion to your son. If he has a genuine talent and interest in this area, you may want to explore the possibility of signing him up for calligraphy lessons. Meanwhile, encourage him to help you with addressing greeting cards, invitations, and so on—opportunities to show off his skill.

How to raise your child's grades in English

The English curriculum (also known as "language" or "language arts") may include language mechanics, handwriting, spelling, and composition. It varies greatly from school to school and from text to text. As a result, there are no blanket remedies for children who experience difficulty in this area.

If your child is earning low grades in English, schedule a conference with the teacher. Let the teacher know that you want to help your child, and ask for suggestions and recommendations. Inquire about state minimum requirements and skills that must be mastered for yearly tests (often called "benchmarks"). "How to improve your child's composition" on pages 71–74 includes many suggestions you should find helpful as you work with your child.

HELP!

"My son has not passed a single English test this year! He never seems to know when tests are scheduled, and he never brings his book home to study. How can I possibly help him?"

Most English books don't conform to the same neat "one-lesson-a-week, test-every-Friday" format as spelling texts. Some lessons may last for less than a week; others may take up to two weeks or more of class time. Find out from your son's teacher how lessons are set up in the text and when tests are scheduled. Ask for extra practice activities and materials your son can complete at home prior to the tests.

"My daughter usually performs well in language arts, but she has real trouble with punctuation. She failed the last three tests and will probably get a C for this grading period. Should I just forget about this problem and assume that her grade will improve as soon as the class moves on to a new unit?"

Even though your daughter's overall grade may be respectable, it's never a good idea to "skip over" an entire set of skills. Knowing how to punctuate is essential, and if she doesn't learn it now, she will have to learn it later. (Punctuation skills are often included on basic skills tests.) Ask the teacher for extra practice activities and materials your daughter can complete at home. Also find out which punctuation skills are included on basic skills tests your daughter will take this year; at the very least, she should master these.

"My son is a whiz in English. His grades have been top-notch all year. But he never brings his book home, so I don't know what he's studying. How can I be sure that he's learning all the skills he needs to score well on our state's basic skills test?"

Talk to the teacher or the academic advisor at your school. Find out how the classroom curriculum correlates with your state's basic skills test. Most schools are very conscious of state requirements and have planned their lessons to promote success on basic skills tests. A conference should provide you with the information you need to feel comfortable about this.

How to improve your child's composition

Perhaps the most important qualification you can bring to this task is. . . patience. Often children (and adults) are anxious to complete a written task and are satisfied with just one draft. If children can learn the value of the pre-writing-writing-revising process at an early age, their writing will be greatly improved for now and in the future. We recommend these steps:

1. Brainstorm.

Before actually beginning a composition, your child should be encouraged to *brainstorm*—to generate and list ideas. You can participate, too, as long as you play equal roles. In other words, a brainstorming session is not the time to exercise your parental authority or to insist that your ideas are the "right" ones.

Brainstorming is used in classrooms, companies, and businesses across the country to promote creative thinking and problem-solving. Fun for all, it has only three simple rules:

▶ Everyone tries to generate as many ideas as possible—from serious to outrageous and everything in between.

▶ Any idea is considered acceptable during the brainstorming session. (Save the weeding out for later.)

▶ No one is allowed to criticize anyone else's ideas.

The more ideas are generated, the more successful the session will be. If your child's writing skills are not at the point where he can write quickly, then you should assume responsibility for listing the ideas as they're spoken.

What kinds of ideas can help with a composition assignment? For example, if your child's assignment is to "describe your favorite person," he can brainstorm characteristics of the person chosen and reasons why that person is worth writing about.

2. Organize.

Once enough ideas have been generated, your child should organize them in a logical order. A formal outline may not be necessary, but some effort should be made to arrange the details in some kind of sequence.

3. Write the first draft.

After the general sequence has been determined, your child should write a *rough* first draft. Pay no attention at this stage to the fine points of spelling or punctuation; the purpose of the first draft is to get something (anything!) down on the page.

4. Revise.

Revisions not only take patience; they also require attention to detail. It's hard at first for young writers to revise their own work because they have not yet internalized grammar rules, and they may not see their own spelling mistakes.

The "A-OK" method is one way to make revising easier and more efficient. It directs the child to focus on one aspect of the composition at a time. Introduce it by modeling—taking your child through each step and showing how it's done. Eventually he should be able to handle it independently.

A-OK has five steps: "MOK," "POK," "SOK," "WOK," and "NOK." Each step contains two or more questions for your child to ask. How much revising is necessary depends on how your child answers the questions.

A-OK*

   I. MOK ("<u>M</u>eaning <u>OK</u>")

- "Does it make sense?"
- "Are my facts correct?"
- "Did I say what I really wanted to say?"

  II. POK ("<u>P</u>aragraph <u>OK</u>")

- "Is it indented?"
- "Is it made up of sentences related to ONE main idea?"
- "Is it connected logically with paragraphs that come before and after?"

 III. SOK ("<u>S</u>entence <u>OK</u>")

- "Does it start with a capital letter?"
- "Does it end with the correct punctuation mark?"
- "Does it express a complete thought?"

 IV. WOK ("<u>W</u>ord <u>OK</u>")

- "Is it spelled correctly?"
- "Is it capitalized correctly (if it needs to be)?"

---

* Adapted from "A-OK: A Reading for Revision Strategy" by Jeanne Shay Schumm in *Reading: Exploration and Discovery*, Vol. 10, No. 1 (Fall 1987).

- "Is it the *very best* word, or is there another, better word
  I could use in its place?"

V. **NOK ("<u>N</u>eatness <u>OK</u>")**

- "Is it easy to read?"
- "Does it follow the format required by my teacher?" (Typed or word processed? Written on every other line or double spaced? Written on one side of the paper only? In a folder?)

Revising is one step of the writing process that is greatly simplified with a word processor. Children who are reluctant to revise on paper may be much more willing to do so when each revision doesn't involve a complete rewrite. With the freedom a word processor provides, and the extra work it saves, even children who don't like to write turn out better papers. For more information on word processing, see Chapter 8.

One final note: Whenever possible, reading for revisions should be done out loud. Errors are easier to catch when they are said and heard than when they are read silently.

HELP!

"My daughter's stories seem more like lists of words than paragraphs. There's no capitalization or punctuation. She's in fourth grade; shouldn't her composition skills be better than this?"

Your daughter could benefit from regular writing practice. Start by giving her short but interesting things to write—postcards to friends or relatives, invitations, descriptions of her favorite TV shows, and so on. Begin working on the sentence level. Show your daughter that each sentence begins with a capital letter and ends with a punctuation mark. After she writes a sentence, have her read it out loud and revise it using the appropriate steps of the A-OK method.

As she becomes more comfortable with her writing, encourage her to move on to longer, more sophisticated sentences. Demonstrate with a basic sentence, then slowly add and edit words to embellish it. *Example:*

"I saw a girl."

"I saw a <u>little</u> girl."

"I saw a <u>happy little</u> girl."

"I <u>noticed</u> a happy little girl <u>wearing red overalls</u>."

"I noticed a happy little girl wearing red overalls <u>and skating backwards down the sidewalk</u>."

Once your daughter feels confident about "SOKing" and "WOKing" sentences, she'll be ready to progress to the paragraph level and from there to more complex compositions.

"My son writes interesting compositions and stories for school, but his grades are never very good because his spelling is poor. I can't figure out why he misspells words in compositions that he has spelled correctly on spelling tests."

Chances are your son's imagination is working faster than his pencil. He's concerned with ideas over form. Congratulate him on his creativity, and let it continue to run free—on the first draft. Then insist that he use the A-OK method to revise it before he hands it in for a grade. (You may need to go through these steps with him several times before he can do them by himself.) Meanwhile, have him keep a list of his misspelled words. He will become aware of which words he is missing, and you can take this opportunity to help him to learn to spell them correctly. Look back at pages 61–64 for suggestions.

If your son consistently has problems spelling while writing, you may want to consider adding this book to the reference library in his study center: the *Bad Speller's Dictionary* by Joseph Krevitsky and Jordan L. Linfield (New York: Random House, 1995).

"My daughter always receives high grades on her compositions. She seems to have a real talent for writing. What can I do to encourage her?"

You can introduce her to ways she might win prizes for her writing or get published. Many civic organizations sponsor writing competitions; check with the teacher, media specialist, or children's librarian. Many publications, local and national, provide space in their issues for children's writing (and some are entirely child-written). A list of publications is found on pages 75–76.

If your daughter seems interested in submitting her work for publication, take her to the library for an afternoon of exploring those magazines the library subscribes to. To see copies of the others, write to the publishers and request samples. (You may be charged a small fee.) Help your daughter examine these thoroughly to determine what kinds of writing get published. Then let *her* decide if she wants to give it a try. Bolster her confidence when and if she receives rejection notices—and tell her to keep trying.

You can also encourage her to share her writing with family and friends. For example, she could make books of her short stories or poems and give them as gifts on special occasions.

Publications and Publishers
That Accept Works by Young Writers

"Think & Grin." *Boys' Life.* Boy Scouts of America, 1325 Walnut Hill Lane, Irving, TX 75015-2079. Ages 8–17. Jokes written on postcards.

Child Life. 1100 Waterway Boulevard, Indianapolis, IN 46206. Ages 10–12. Short stories (1,000 words) and poetry.

Cricket Submissions. Carus Publishing Company, 315 Fifth Street, P.O. Box 300, Peru, IL 61354. Ages 7–14. Poetry, stories, and art for contests. Submissions must be accompanied by a statement signed by a teacher or parent assuring that the child's work is original and that no help was given.

New Moon: The Magazine for Girls and Their Dreams. P.O. Box 3587, Duluth, MN 55803-3587. Ages 10–15. Letters, news about girls and women, "herstory" articles about girls and women from the past, articles about girls and women of today doing great things, letters about unfair things that happen to girls just because they're girls, reviews, poetry, drawings, quotes, and more. Submission guidelines on the WWW: http://www.newmoon.duluth.mn.us/~newmoon/girlguid.html

Shoe Tree: The Literary Magazine By and For Children. P.O. Box 452, Belvidere, NJ 07823. Ages 5–14. A quarterly published by the National Association for Young Writers, "Helping Children Write to the Top." All stories, poems, and artwork are done by children. Holds annual competitions for young writers in fiction, poetry, and nonfiction.

Skipping Stones. P.O. Box 3939, Eugene, OR 97403-0939. Ages 8–18. An international multicultural children's magazine that encourages an understanding of different cultures and languages, with an emphasis on ecology and human relationships. Includes artwork, writings, riddles, book reviews, news items, and a pen pal section; accepts work by children from around the world. English and Spanish/English editions.

Stone Soup. P.O. Box 83, Santa Cruz, CA 95063. Ages 8–13. "The magazine by young writers and artists" publishes stories, poems, book reviews, and art by children and adolescents. Submission guidelines on the WWW: http://www.stonesoup.com/guidelines.html

Other possibilities for young authors include:

National Written & Illustrated By. . . Awards Contest for Students. Landmark Editions, Inc., 1402 Kansas Avenue, Kansas City, MO 64127. Publishes books by young authors in three age categories: 6–9, 10–13, 14–19. Each entry must be written and illustrated by the same student. For complete rules and guidelines, send a self-addressed, stamped, business-size envelope with two first-class stamps.

Tyketoon Young Author Publishing Company. 7414 Douglas Lane, Fort Worth, TX 76180. Publishes approximately one book each year by a young author at each grade level from 1–8. Authors and illustrators receive cash scholarships paid as a royalty on each book sold.

For more information on publications that accept work by young writers, contests for young writers, and advice for aspiring authors ages 12 and up, see:

The Young Person's Guide to Becoming a Writer by Janet E. Grant (Minneapolis: Free Spirit Publishing, 1995).

Finally, the Internet offers many opportunities for young people to publish their writing. For an excellent list of links to online publications for (and often by) children, go to: http://www.yahooligans.com/Entertainment/Magazines/

How to Help Your Child with Math

"I hear and I forget.
I see and I remember.
I do and I understand."

Chinese proverb

What's new in math instruction?

You might also ask, "Where were the calculators when I was in school?" And you might observe, "Math class sure has changed!" In fact, mathematics instruction has been in a state of flux for several years. Why? First of all, technology is changing. The increasing availability of calculators and computers has diminished the need for human beings to do low-level calculations. Second, job demands are more often related to higher-level thinking and decision-making than low-level calculations.

The National Council of Teachers of Mathematics (NCTM) has played a strong leadership role throughout this process. In 1989, NCTM adopted a new set of Curriculum and Evaluation Standards for School Mathematics. These standards have four major themes: problem solving, communication, reasoning, and connections. In other words, mathematics is now seen as a way for human beings to solve problems, to communicate with each other about ideas, and to engage in logical reasoning. Moreover, mathematics is linked more clearly to the real world than it was when we adults were in school.

What does a math class look like today? Chances are your child will still learn basic calculation skills, but those skills will be balanced with the curriculum goals set forth by NCTM. Even elementary curriculum is likely to include areas previously saved for high school, such as basic algebra. Your child won't use just a pencil and paper for mathematics; he or she will also use a computer, a calculator, and lots of hands-on manipulative materials. Furthermore, the myth that "math is for boys" has largely been dispelled, so both girls and boys will be encouraged to excel in mathematics.

Because the nature of mathematics instruction has changed so radically since we were students, you'll want to become familiar with the curriculum and teaching procedures at your child's school. Here are some questions to guide your discussion with the teacher:

> ▶ "Please tell me about the math curriculum. In what ways is my child learning about calculation, problem solving, communication, reasoning, and connecting math to the real world?"

> ▶ "How are students grouped for math instruction?"

> ▶ "How are computers and calculators used in the classroom?"

> ▶ "How is my child's progress in math monitored?"

> ▶ "How will I be informed if my child is falling behind in math?"

> ▶ "How can I support the math program by helping out at home?"

 **HELP!**

"My son is in third grade. At the beginning of the school year, we received a list of school supplies we needed to buy. A calculator was on the list. I'm worried that my son won't learn his math facts."

In the past, so much attention was placed on computation that there was insufficient time left over for learning math skills such as solving word problems and applying mathematics to solve real-world problems. To improve the use of instructional time, NCTM recommends that children learn to use calculators at a very young age. There is no research suggesting that the use of calculators inhibits one's learning of basic math operations. Don't worry; your son's teacher is preparing him for the future!

"My daughter keeps talking about 'estimating' answers. What's wrong with getting the *right* answers? I don't understand the emphasis on estimation."

In everyday mathematics, there are times when we need an exact answer, and times when an approximate answer will do. When you're at the store, in the workplace, or in a discussion with a family member, you may need to do some speedy mental arithmetic to make a decision or respond to a comment or observation. *Examples:* "There's 20 percent more in the bottle, and it costs a dollar more. . . is it a bargain?" "Do I really agree with the proposal for the new retirement plan?" "Let's see; two dollars more allowance per week equals how much more per year?"

Knowing how to estimate is a real-life, real-world skill. Also, children who are good at estimating are able to quickly realize when an answer is way off base and rule out some incorrect choices on standardized achievement tests. If exact answers are needed, they can use calculators or pencil-and-paper.

Rest assured that your daughter *is* learning and *will* learn how to arrive at exact answers to problems. She's probably learning multiple ways to solve problems for different purposes. Talk to the teacher to find out how estimating and mental arithmetic fit into the curriculum.

"I've heard that math instruction has changed, but I can tell you one thing that *hasn't* changed: Math was and is my worst subject! My palms still sweat when I think about math tests, and now it's the same for my daughter. She's a basket case on test days. How can I help her?"

Math anxiety is very real. Children and adults with math anxiety become extremely fearful of mathematics and avoid it as much as possible. Talk with your daughter's teacher and, if necessary, the school counselor. Enlist their help. In the meantime, you might compile a mental list of real-life, everyday situations where you use math. It makes a difference when we realize that math is simply a tool to help us make decisions and solve real-life problems. Also point out any instances you observe where your daughter uses math without anxiety. *Examples:* Figuring out if she has enough money to pay for a movie and popcorn; deciding whether her bed will fit in a corner or be too big; planning the time she'll need to complete a long-term project or report.

How to help your child with math concepts

Like math facts, math concepts should be taught in logical sequences. Start by familiarizing yourself with your child's math text so you can understand its sequence of instruction. Check with the teacher to find out if he will be using the materials in a different sequence or supplementing them with others. The more informed you are, the more you will be able to help your child.

Addition, subtraction, multiplication, division, fractions, and decimals

Any learning is easier with concrete aids. Start with body parts (like fingers and toes), follow with other concrete objects (like pennies and buttons), and end up with abstract numbers, and you'll have made these basic concepts much more accessible to your child.

Children need to understand that addition and subtraction are opposite operations, as are multiplication and division. They also need to understand that multiplication is a fast way of adding, and that division is a fast way of subtracting. Proving answers by performing opposite operations can help bring home these concepts.

The concept of decimals is best taught with money. Using coins and bills to indicate the difference between $0.50, $5.00, and $50.00 can make light bulbs go on over children's heads. Once children have learned decimals with money, it's easy for them to understand decimals overall.

Fractions can be more difficult to grasp. A child may quite reasonably wonder how 1/5 can be smaller than 1/4, since five is more than four. Or, when one of three parts of a circle is colored in, why is this part 1/3 instead of 1/2, since one part is colored in and two parts aren't? Use concrete aids—slices of cake, measuring spoons, rulers, fraction puzzle pieces—to help your child "see" these concepts.

Money

Money concepts can be taught in a variety of ways. Children especially enjoy having and using their own money in practice sessions and games—as long as you promise to give it all back at the end! Here are some ideas to try with your child:

- ▶ Give your child an allowance and have her open a savings account.
- ▶ Play *Monopoly*—a great favorite among even young children. As their grasp of basic math concepts improves, they can be allowed to act as the Banker.
- ▶ Practice making change. Start by teaching your child to "count up" from the cost of the item being purchased (at a real store or a "pretend store"). Children should learn to count up to coin amounts first, then to single dollars, and finally to multiple dollar bills. Try the following tips for teaching these skills:

- If the cost ends in a number other than 5 or 0, use pennies until you reach a number that ends with 5 or 0.
- If the cost ends in 5 or 0, use nickels and dimes until you reach 25, 50, or 75.
- If the cost ends in 25, 50, or 75, use quarters until you reach 100 (one dollar).

You can also use money to begin teaching an older child about percentages. Toys are usually taxed. Help your child figure out the actual cost of a toy she wants to purchase by estimating the tax that will be added at the checkout counter. *Example:* "The game you want costs $4.75. The tax is five percent—that's five cents added to every dollar. $4.75 is almost $5.00. Five dollars times five cents equals 25 cents. Now add that to $4.75. The real price of your game will be just about $5.00."

Time

Children naturally develop a sense of time as they grow. Young children initially perceive no difference between a week and a year. (The day following one birthday, they're likely to ask how soon they can expect the next.) This is one reason why children have so little patience when it comes to waiting for anticipated events. Anything more distant than tomorrow seems impossibly far away.

▶ Have your child mark off days on a calendar. She will gradually come to understand how much time a week takes, and that's a step in the direction of comprehending the length of a month and even a year.

▶ Be sure to have at least one non-digital (analog) clock in the house. If your clock has a second hand, that's even better. The movement of a second hand is something a child can see.

▶ Buy your child a toy clock or a non-digital watch, then teach her to tell time in the following sequence: hour, half-hour, quarter-hour, and finally five- and then one-minute intervals. Gradually introduce the different terms for the same concepts: "three-thirty" (easier) and "half past three" (harder), "four forty-five" (easier) and "a quarter to five" (harder). Pay special attention to troublesome areas. For example, children have a tendency to read 7:50 as 8:50 because the hour hand is closer to the 8 than the 7.

Geometry and measurement

Again, use concrete aids. To a child, seeing is believing, and touching is even more convincing.

- ▶ Have your child build a birdhouse or other object that requires accurate measurement and may also necessitate an understanding of perimeter, area, and other concepts.

- ▶ Let your child plot her growth on a wall chart (or make pencil marks along a doorjamb).

- ▶ Invite your child to help you make cookies. She can read the recipe, assist with measuring out dry ingredients, read the marks on the butter wrapper, and lick the spoon.

We could list dozens more suggestions—having your child read her weight on a scale, giving your child responsibility for reading the temperature on the thermometer each morning before school (and dressing accordingly), letting her use tools (with supervision), and so on. Draw on your own imagination and the tasks of your daily life to come up with others that will interest your child.

Incidentally, it's a *very* good idea to teach metric along with English measures (English measures being the ones Americans normally use: foot, inch, ounce, pound, etc.). The metric system is the standard in most countries, and while an effort to educate the American public (through road signs showing both miles and kilometers, for example) has largely been ignored, your child will probably need to know both.

How to help your child with word problems

The purpose of most word problems is to apply math concepts to real-life situations. Many children have a hard time puzzling through the prose to find the numbers they need. The "SIR RIGHT" method can help, although some steps will be unnecessary for some problems. Teach it by modeling it for your child with one or more homework problems.

Start by reading the problem silently to get a general understanding of it.

Identify all numbers written as digits or words. It may be necessary to look for "hidden" numbers ("dozen," "half as many," and so on).

Read the problem again, this time out loud, and draw a picture or diagram of it. (Some children may be able to do this in their heads.)

Read the problem yet again to find out what it is asking for. The answer may involve working backward from the question. (As many children have discovered, it's easier to solve a maze by starting at the Finish.)

Inquire, "What do I have to do to answer the problem?" Remember to add or multiply if a larger number is expected, or to subtract or divide if a smaller number is expected. Look for key words that tell you which operation is correct. *Examples:*

- "Total," "in all," and "altogether" indicate the need for addition or multiplication.
- "How much is left," "how many are left," "how many more/greater/less than," and "how much older than" indicate the need for subtraction.
- "How much. . . each" and "how many. . . each" indicate the need for division.

Give the problem smaller numbers than the ones actually used in it. If you are still puzzled by the problem, repeat the Read and Inquire steps.

Ham it up, acting out the problem if necessary.

Take a pencil and solve the problem, check your computation, and make sure that the answer makes sense.

Of course, you can also use real-life situations to make word problems more attractive to your child. Instead of asking, "If Johnny has two bananas and four friends to share them with, what should he do?" give your child two bananas the next time four friends come over and have him figure it out.

Finally, have your child make up word problems that are personally interesting to him. Problems about Ninja turtles, trading cards, TV or movie stars, or hobbies are sure to be more fascinating than the ones in the math book. Research has shown that this practice helps students solve word problems on standardized tests.

 **HELP!**

"My son simply cannot solve word problems. Other than that, his math homework is fine. He can read the problems, but if more than one computation process is required, he's lost."

Teach him the "SIR RIGHT" method explained above. Work through it with him until he is able to act independently.

"My daughter is a poor reader and has trouble with word problems as a result. Should I read them out loud to her?"

It would be wise to discuss this with the teacher. If the teacher approves, you can read the problems to your daughter so she won't miss out on math concepts because of her reading difficulties. The teacher may be willing to make special arrangements for her during tests involving word problems.

"My son is a sixth grader who usually has no trouble with math. But he's having problems understanding and using the metric system. I don't understand it very well myself. How can I help?"

If you aren't familiar with the metric system, take this opportunity to learn it with your child. The relationships within the metric system are easy to follow because they are based on the decimal system.

The units of length, weight, and capacity are the *meter*, *gram*, and *liter*, respectively. The prefixes *deci-*, *centi-*, and *milli-* refer to 1/10, 1/100, and 1/1,000 of a unit. The prefixes *deca-*, *hecto-*, and *kilo-* refer to 10, 100, and 1,000 units.

Your son may be having trouble making mental images of metric measurements. Most people, when they think about a gallon, picture a gallon of milk. Help your son come up with similar images for the metric system. *Examples:*

- ▶ A centimeter may be about the size of the fingernail on his thumb.
- ▶ A liter is a little more than a quart, or half the size of a large-size bottle of Coca-Cola.
- ▶ A gram is about the weight of a large paper clip.

Comparative images like these will be most effective if your son is the one who comes up with them.

How to help your child with math facts and computation

A child who knows math facts can instantly give answers to addition, subtraction, multiplication, and division number sentences in which two of the numbers are generally one-digit numbers. (*Examples:* 3 + 6, 7 − 2, 8 x 8, 49 ÷ 9.) Before you start teaching math facts to your child, check with the teacher to find out the sequence of lessons for the year. Look through your child's math book when he brings it home, and preview the pages to be learned or worked on before beginning each homework session. Don't encourage your child to work ahead in the book without getting prior approval from the teacher.

▸ As a general rule, teach math facts using low numbers first. There are exceptions; for example, the multiplication tables which are easiest to teach (and learn) are the 0's, 1's, 2's, 5's, 10's, and 11's.

▸ Use "skip counting"—for example, counting by 2's or 3's—when helping a child learn multiplication. One of the best tools we've found for teaching this technique is an audiocassette called "Skip Count Kid and Friends: Musical Multiplication Tape." Write to: James R. McGhee II, 8200 SW 130 Street, Miami, FL 33156.

▸ Teach related math facts together. For example, "3 + 5" should be taught with "5 + 3," and "8 – 3" should be taught with "8 – 5." Practice gained by filling in addition and multiplication tables can help children discover some of these relationships. See pages 172 and 173 for grids you can copy and use.

▸ Teach math facts in small doses. As a rule of thumb, three new facts are sufficient for one session.

▸ Use different formats when teaching math facts. Your child should be able to recognize the same fact regardless of how it's presented. Mix-and-match these methods:

● Present the problem orally. (Ask "What's 3 + 4?)

● Write the problem vertically:

$$
\begin{array}{r}
3 \\
+\ \ 4 \\
\hline
7
\end{array}
$$

● Write the problem horizontally:

$3 + 4 = 7$

● Alternate between writing on paper and writing on flash cards or on a slate.

▸ Experiment with possibilities. *Example:* "How many ways can we make 7? There's 3 + 4, and 21 ÷ 3, and 10 – 3, and 7 x 1, and on and on and on. . . ."

▸ Review math facts with your child often. Frequent short sessions (10 minutes or so) are usually more effective than infrequent long sessions.

We recommend that you start helping your child to *overlearn* math facts as soon as they are introduced in class. Often, parents wait until after their child's teacher says that the child is experiencing difficulty. While it's never too late, it's certainly simpler and more pleasant to exercise preventive teaching.

Even after your child appears to know and understand the math facts appropriate to his grade level, they should still be practiced frequently. Aim to "program" them into your child's brain so thoroughly that he can answer problems without having to figure them out.

In helping your child with computation, note the following pointers:

▶ Familiarize yourself with the procedures your child is being taught in school so you don't inadvertently confuse him by using other procedures. For example, in long division, the teacher may want the children to fill in 0's where you were taught to leave empty spaces, like this:

$$
\begin{array}{r}
98 \\
18)\overline{1764} \\
\underline{1620} \\
144 \\
\underline{144} \\
000
\end{array}
$$

▶ Some teachers require children to copy problems before working them (a practice we recommend over simply filling in blanks on worksheets). Have your child check to see that problems were copied correctly.

▶ Don't let your child practice a mathematical operation incorrectly. If he's getting wrong answers, ask him to explain how he arrived at the answers. This should help you determine the underlying cause for the difficulty. Possible causes might include:

• insufficient knowledge of math facts

• carelessness, and

• poor understanding of the computation process.

If poor understanding turns out to be the cause, ask the teacher for suggestions. (Make sure that *you* understand the process being taught at school.) Or have your child leave that page or assignment undone. Write a note to the teacher explaining what you think is the source of the problem. This will be a sign to the teacher that further instruction is necessary.

▶ Resist the urge to correct your child's computation errors. Instead, encourage your child to proofread and correct his own problems. Doing the reverse operation is a preferred way of proofreading. *Example:*

$$\begin{array}{r} 42 \\ -19 \\ \hline 23 \end{array} \longleftrightarrow \begin{array}{r} 23 \\ +19 \\ \hline 42 \end{array}$$

When to worry about children who count on their fingers

Imagine learning to bake a cake without actually doing it. Consider telling someone how to tie a pair of shoelaces without demonstrating it. These tasks would be difficult, if not impossible! So it's understandable that young children in particular need concrete aids when learning math facts and computation. And if there's one thing they can always count on to be there for them, it's their own ten fingers.

The age at which children outgrow counting on their fingers varies from child to child. If your child is still doing it by the third or fourth grade, talk to the teacher and find out what other aids are available. This is especially important if the teacher penalizes children for counting on their fingers.

Making math fun

There are many fun and interesting ways to practice math facts and computation; see Chapter 9 for suggestions. You may want to purchase one or more of the commercial games that teach or reinforce these skills, such as *Yahtzee* or *Milles Bornes.* Flash cards and computer software are other options for you to explore.

Whenever possible, these skills should be taught in meaningful, real-life contexts. Supervise your child as she makes a minor purchase at a store and keeps the change (counting it afterward to make sure it's right). Open a savings account for your child at a local bank. Let your child take her weekly allowance out of a pile of coins. You can probably think of dozens more ways to bring math into your daily activities with your child.

There are also several "tricks" that can take the drudgery out of math facts and computation. (Plus these can serve as a source of pride for your child, since other children may not know them.) *Example:* You might lead your child to discover that adding 9 is the same as adding 10 and taking away 1, or that subtracting 9 is the same as subtracting 10 and adding 1.

Following are more tricks to try with your child.

For teaching fraction reductions and division

▶ Numbers that end in a multiple of 2 are divisible by 2. *Examples:* 4, 38, 576, even 1,395,405,778.

▶ Numbers whose last two digits are a multiple of 4, or whose last three digits are a multiple of 8, are divisible by 4 and 8, respectively. *Example:* Since 56 is divisible by 4, so is 1,356.

▶ Numbers whose digits add up to multiples of 3 or 9 are divisible by 3 or 9, respectively. *Example:* The digits in 378 add up to 18. Since 18 is divisible by both 3 and 9, so is 378.

▶ Numbers that end in 5 or 0 are divisible by 5.

▶ Numbers that end in 0 are divisible by 10.

For teaching multiplication

The "Nines Trick" works for the nines tables. Model it for your child, who will probably be eager to imitate you.

1. Number your fingers from 1–10.

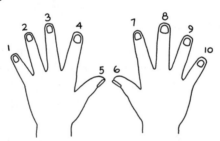

2. Let's say that the problem you want to demonstrate is 9 x 7. Flex the 7 finger. Everything to the *left* of that finger is the tens; everything to the *right* of that finger is the ones. There are 6 fingers to the left and 3 fingers to the right, so the product is 63.

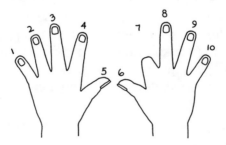

3. This trick can also be used for division when the divisor is 9. For example, to find the answer to 63 ÷ 9, flex the finger that would separate 6 tens from 3 ones. That would be the 7 finger, making the quotient 7.

   The "Sluggard's Rule" works when both factors are from 6–10 inclusive. (This trick, also called "finger multiplication," was introduced by Dantzig in 1941.) It's more difficult than the "Nines Trick" and should be taught only after that trick has been mastered. Your child will need to know the multiplication tables up through 4 x 4 in order to use this trick. Again, you should model it for your child, not just describe it.

   1. Start by numbering the fingers on each of your hands from 6–10, beginning with the thumbs.

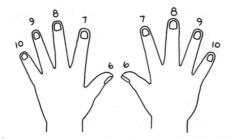

   2. To find the product of 8 x 7, touch the 8 finger of one hand to the 7 finger of the other hand. Flex the fingers numbered higher than the two that are touching (the 9 and 10, and the 8, 9, and 10.

   3. Add the number of the *outstretched* fingers (including the two that are touching) to get the tens. Multiply the number of *flexed* fingers on one hand by the number of *flexed* fingers on the other hand to get the ones. In this example, 3 + 2 = 5 for the tens, and 2 x 3 = 6 for the ones, making the product 56.

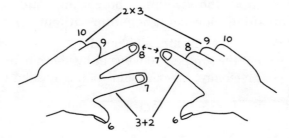

   4. For 6 x 6 and 7 x 6, a bit of extra computation is necessary. With 6 x 6 there would be one finger *up* on each hand, making two tens (1 + 1). Then

there would be four fingers *flexed* on each hand, making the ones' product 16. This product must be added to the 20 (two tens) for the tens, making the final product 20 + 16 = 36.

This "Sluggard's Rule" may seem complicated, but never underestimate the child who is desperate to find some "magical" way of figuring out multiplication facts.

 **HELP!**

"My daughter is a fifth grader who doesn't know her multiplication facts. She takes forever to do her homework. Should I let her use a calculator?"

First, find out if her teacher has a plan for helping students master multiplication facts. If so, you can reinforce it at home. If the teacher isn't using a particular plan, have your daughter practice with flash cards. Meanwhile, you can let her use a calculator for long multiplication problems. This will enable her to concentrate on the process without being held back by her lack of knowledge. Once she understands the process, she can return to multiplying on her own and use the calculator to check her answers.

Most children would prefer to do *all* of their math homework on a calculator—not because they're lazy (although this may sometimes be the case), but also because calculators are fun to use. Some children will spend blissful hours punching numbers in and watching them appear on the display. To reinforce learning during play, you may want to provide a calculator that functions like an adding machine, printing out whole problems as well as the answers.

"My son needs a lot of help with his math homework, but the terms used in his text are different from the ones I learned when I was in school. I'm discovering, for example, that 'trading,' 'borrowing,' and 'regrouping' can all mean the same thing. How can I help him without confusing him?"

If your son can't define the terms himself, you may be able to check their meanings by looking at the sample problems in his math book or checking the glossary. For your reference, here are some of the most basic terms:

addend	factor
+ <u>addend</u>	x <u>factor</u>
sum	product

$$
\begin{array}{l}
\text{minuend} \\
\underline{-\ \text{subtrahend}} \\
\text{difference}
\end{array}
\qquad
\begin{array}{r}
\underline{\text{quotient}}\ (+\ \text{remainder}) \\
\text{divisor}\ )\ \text{dividend}
\end{array}
$$

"My son's math homework is sloppy. Since he doesn't line up his numbers correctly, he makes mistakes with two-digit addition and subtraction problems."

Have his vision checked by an ophthalmologist or optometrist; his problem may be visual. Or he may be working too fast and may simply need to slow down. If his problem is severe, let him use graph paper with large squares, or turn his regular writing paper around so the lines are vertical rather than horizontal. Then have him write numbers between the lines, as in the example shown below. After completing his homework, he can copy the problems on clean paper in the standard fashion.

$$
\begin{array}{c|c|c}
 & 3 & 4 \\
+ & 4 & 6 \\
\hline
 & 8 & 0 \\
\end{array}
$$

"My daughter does well in math, but she sometimes makes careless errors. What can I do?"

Your daughter should get in the habit of proofreading her work. If she can't spot errors when going over the problems, she can redo them on a separate sheet of paper.

Or she can perform the opposite operation and compare her results. For example, a division problem can be proved by multiplying the quotient times the divisor and adding any remainder to obtain the dividend. If the problem is to divide 47 by 7 and she comes up with this answer:

$$
\begin{array}{r}
6,\ \text{remainder } 5 \\
7)\overline{\ 47} \\
\underline{42} \\
5
\end{array}
$$

she can check it with this computation:

$$(6 \times 7) + 5 = 47$$

Both redoing problems and performing opposite operations are repetitive and time-consuming tasks. Either may teach your daughter to be more careful the first time around.

How to Help Your Child with Science, Social Studies, and Foreign Languages

"I wanted to know the name of every stone and flower
and insect and bird and beast. I wanted to know
where it got its color, where it got its life—
but there was no one to tell me."

George Washington Carver

What's new in science and social studies instruction?

When you were in school, science and social studies probably meant learning facts from a textbook and an encyclopedia. In social studies, for example, you might have learned all of the state capitals but not how to find the states on a map, much less how to understand the interplay among the geographic, economic, historical, cultural, and social factors that define a state or region. Many teachers today focus more on this broader picture. Another example of the broadening scope of social studies is increased emphasis—even in the early grades—on principles of economics.

There is also a greater awareness of and sensitivity to diversity and multiculturalism. When we adults were in school, traditional methods of teaching about other countries and cultures often resulted in our seeing them only as curiosities. (*Example:* We learned to picture children from the Netherlands as all wearing wooden shoes!) Teachers are moving now to pluralistic approaches that teach children we are all members of varied cultures. Thus, a child who is a female, Catholic, Italian-American, and midwesterner learns that she is a member of many cultures. This approach helps children understand and celebrate our similarities as well as our differences.

Social studies and science instruction is also moving beyond what you may remember as grades based on the "right" answer. Teachers now focus not only on a right answer (the product), but also on the process—how you arrived at that answer. Thus, you may see your child spend more science time involved in experiments that help him to understand the scientific process—the "hows" and "what ifs." These emerging changes in science and social studies are backed by national professional organizations which are developing national standards to guide instruction.

How these changes are reflected in homework

Taken together, these changes are likely to mean:

> ▸ *less* homework from textbooks, *more* experiments and projects

> ▸ *less* memorization of facts, *more* focus on understanding concepts, and

> ▸ *less* emphasis on the idiosyncrasies of various cultures, *more* emphasis on the interdependence of world cultures.

Beyond the three R's

Learning how to learn about science and social studies requires completely different strategies than those needed for reading, writing, and arithmetic—the three R's considered basic to education. Yet success in science and social studies depends on how well your child has mastered those skills.

Some children who breeze through the three R's have difficulty with science and social studies. This may be due to a lack of interest, or it may depend on how comfortable a child feels with the way science and social studies texts are written and organized. For girls, it may be due to a lack of expectation that they will achieve in science. It isn't uncommon for children to perform differently in each subject area. In other words, if your child is brilliant in math, don't assume that he or she will be equally brilliant in science. (That's equivalent to telling someone, "You can type, so you should be able to play the piano.")

How to help your child with read-the-chapter, answer-the-questions assignments

As early as third grade, children may be required to read chapters in science or social studies books and answer the questions following the chapters. (Or the teacher may substitute or supplement with other questions.) For children who are accustomed to reading primarily fiction—whether children's literature or the stories in their basal readers—this may prove to be a tedious task.

Reading informational material takes a whole new approach. Among other differences, it requires reading for facts as well as theme, and reading more slowly so as not to miss anything important. Informational material tends to be written more densely and may be written at a higher reading level than fiction intended for the same grade. And, frankly, it's often not written very well. It may be grammatically accurate but not very "considerate" of the reader.

The usual purpose of read-the-chapter, answer-the-questions exercises is to train children to study a body of information for testing at a later date. The following four-step strategy is designed to help your child become comfortable with this process. Start by reading it aloud to your child (including the "Caution" at the end) and modeling it until he gains confidence and proficiency. (For a slightly different approach, look back at pages 53–55.)

1. **Preview the chapter.** Skim through it quickly before actually starting to read it. Previewing means:

   ▶ reading the chapter headings and subheadings

   ▶ reading the introduction

   ▶ reading the summary at the end

   ▶ looking at graphs, tables, charts, maps, and other illustrations, and

   ▶ checking out features like the index and the glossary, which may guide you to some of the answers you need to find.

Previewing helps you budget your reading time by giving you an idea of how long the chapter is and whether you're familiar with the subject matter. If the chapter is long, you may want to read it in more than one sitting. If it contains many new and difficult words, chunk it into small pieces and tackle them one at a time.

(PARENTS: This step may require some advance preparation. For example, your child may ignore the legend at the bottom of a chart or a map and misunderstand it entirely. Or your child may not understand the purpose of the index or glossary. You may want to begin by paging through the book, pointing out the various parts, and explaining them in simple language.)

2. **Now read the questions.** Read them all the way through, looking up any words you don't understand.

3. **Now read the chapter carefully.**

4. **Now answer the questions, looking back through the chapter whenever you need to.** If you're supposed to write the answers in complete sentences, be sure to check your capitalization and punctuation.

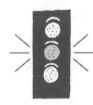

C A U T I O N

DON'T, repeat, DON'T get in the habit of using the "search-and-destroy" approach to these assignments. In other words, DON'T read the questions first and then skim the chapter to find the answers. If you don't give the chapter a THOROUGH reading, you may miss important facts and concepts you need for tests.

 **H E L P !**

"My daughter isn't in the highest reading group in her class, but she still has to use the same science book those students use. There is no way that she can complete her assignments by herself; her reading skills aren't up to it. Should I help her by reading the chapters out loud to her?"

If the text is really too difficult for her, talk to the teacher. If the teacher insists that your daughter participate with the rest of the class in using this text, it may be necessary for you to read the chapters to her.

"My son always get A's on his daily work in history, but he rarely passes the tests. How can he answer questions correctly on his daily work but not remember the answers when test time comes?"

He may be using the "search-and-destroy" method to answer the questions in his daily work. Encourage your son to read the chapter carefully *before* trying to answer the questions. A quick review the night or morning before the test will help, too.

"My son never reads his geography chapter before starting to answer the questions at the end. Yet he seems to get all the answers right, and he also does well on tests. Should I still insist that he read the chapters carefully?"

Perhaps the teacher lectures right from the text or allows class time for reading the chapters. Ask and find out. On the other hand, your son may simply be familiar with the material being covered. As long as he's doing such a good job, let him continue in the same manner. (Remember the old saying: "If it isn't broken, don't fix it!") Keep an eye on him in the future, though, when other teachers' styles may require him to do more work on his own.

How to help your child study chapters for tests

Knowing how to study chapters for tests is vital, since your child will be required to do this through high school and beyond. Relatively few children can read a chapter once and retain all the information needed for a test; most need to practice more intense study methods. Look back at pages 25–27 for suggestions that can help you help your child. Following are more techniques for you to try:

If studying for a test has been preceded by a "read-the-chapter, answer-the questions" exercise, half of the work has been done already. If not, the study session should begin with a preview and careful reading of the chapter, as described on pages 94–95. Even if your child has carefully read the whole chapter once, a methodical rereading may be necessary to prepare for a test. Here is the procedure we recommend:

1. Have your child read each paragraph or section, then stop.
2. Now have your child try to project one or two questions the teacher might possibly ask about the paragraph or section.
3. Record these questions on individual index cards (flash cards), with the answers on the back.
4. After your child has finished rereading the entire chapter, make additional flash cards for any questions at the end of the chapter which cannot be answered immediately.
5. Finally, make flash cards for new vocabulary words introduced in the chapter.

Once these first five steps have been accomplished, the *real* studying can begin:

6. Go over the flash cards until your child knows the answers automatically. Given enough drill-and-practice, her memory should "kick in" even if test anxiety sets in.

7. If you know what format the test will take—matching, fill-in-the-blanks, short answer, and so on—try to construct a sample test with your child. (This can be especially beneficial for children who have high test anxiety.)

This process takes time and commitment on your part and your child's. But our experience as students, teachers, and tutors has convinced us that it *works*—and often results in improved grades.

Making studying fun

Studying for tests will *not* be fun if you and your child start too late. From the very first day of the new school year, emphasize to your child that she *must* let you know about a test as soon as it is announced in class. (You may want to use the Assignment Sheet on page 154 or 155 to record test dates and relevant information.) Once you hear about a test, you and your child can plan your study time accordingly.

Many games can be adapted to studying for chapter tests. See Chapter 9 for suggestions.

 **HELP!**

"There is absolutely no way that my son can make up sample test questions! He has a hard enough time just reading the chapter, much less understanding it well enough to invent questions."

Your son needs you to model this for him. Start by reading the chapter with him, paragraph by paragraph. Then have your son make up a question while you make one up at the same time. Record the questions on flash cards. Don't expect miracles overnight, but your son should gradually become familiar enough with the kinds of questions his teacher asks that he can begin constructing his own.

"My daughter can understand chapter material fairly easily, but her attention span is very short. The night before a test, she is in misery studying the chapters. The chapters are just too long."

Your daughter needs to study well in advance of a test—not only the night before. As soon as a chapter is assigned, have her chunk it into smaller portions, then read and study one portion each night. This eliminates the last-minute cramming routine that most children find frustrating and scary.

"My daughter never needs to study for tests. The most she ever has to do is quickly read over a chapter the night before. I'm afraid that when she encounters more difficult material in college, she will fall apart. Shouldn't she form the habit *now* of studying more carefully?"

Her manner of studying may carry her through college and beyond. However, it isn't uncommon for outstanding high school students to run into trouble later, when they are asked to master more difficult materials. If your daughter is serious about her grades, you may want to enroll her in a study skills course so she will be ready to adjust her study habits if and when this becomes necessary.

How to help your child with graphics

Much of the material in science and social studies texts is presented in the form of maps, charts, timelines, and graphs. Formal instruction in graphics other than maps typically begins in the third grade and continues through junior high school; it may be included as part of the math, reading, science, and/or social studies curriculum. Even so, some children continue to have difficulty interpreting graphics or fail to see their importance. This is especially true if reading is a chore for them. They concentrate so hard on the text that they don't have any energy left over for the graphics.

Map-reading skills may be introduced as early as kindergarten. Instruction usually begins with the concepts of near/far, up/down, and above/below and gradually moves to complex concepts like the International Date Line, map scale, and map projection/distortion. (These are normally covered by the sixth grade.) Often, map concepts take root slowly and are hard for children to grasp. Many third grade students, for example, are amazed to learn that we do not live "inside" the earth. Others regularly confuse cities with states and continents with countries.

One good way to help your child understand graphic materials is through the use of graphs on a computer. Another way is to encourage and assist him in making maps, graphs, timelines, and so on with construction paper, crayons, colorful marker, rulers, and other interesting tools. Hands-on experience is not only fun; it also enables children to comprehend the reasons for graphics and the ways they are produced.

Maps

▸ Find out the sequence of map skills taught in your child's class. If your child is experiencing difficulty, perhaps he hasn't yet mastered the prerequisite skills. Ask the teacher for suggestions you can use at home.

▸ Many children have trouble with the concept of distance. One of us tutored a 10-year-old whose longest on-the-ground "trip" was a five-mile ride from his home to the airport. The idea of driving 100 miles in a car was beyond his comprehension. You can instill a sensitivity to distance with activities like these:

● Walk a mile with your child, then show him how a mile is represented on a map.

● Ask your child to keep track of the odometer reading during car trips. (If you have a "trip meter," set it to 0 at the beginning for an exact count of the miles traveled.) Then show him how that distance is represented on a road map.

● Orient your child to the four cardinal directions. Go outside and point out North, South, East, and West. If you have a compass, use it to demonstrate direction. (You may want to buy your child a compass of his own; kids love gadgets like these.) Be patient when helping your child learn these concepts.

▸ Relative location—the location of one place in relation to another—can also be difficult for children to grasp. Using a map with a compass, ask your child a series of questions like these:

● "What direction is _____ from _____?"

● "Is _____ north or south of _____?"

● "If you were going from _____ to _____, in what direction would you be going?"

▸ Encourage your child to read a map legend carefully before attempting to answer any questions about the map.

▸ Determine the meaning of any other symbols on the map and help your child discover how and where they are used.

▸ Refresh your own knowledge of map-related vocabulary. Your child may be asked to locate a continent, a peninsula, or a strait on a map without having any inkling of what those terms mean.

▸ Keep an atlas and a globe at home (perhaps in your child's study center) and use them frequently—to add meaning to coin and stamp collections, when reading stories about other lands, and so on. If your child has access to a computer and CD-ROM with geographical information, so much the better!

C A U T I O N

If your child is colorblind, he or she may have special difficulty with color-coded maps. Be sure that the teacher is aware of this condition early in the school year.

Graphs, diagrams, and tables

Graphs, diagrams, and tables are common graphics. The following tips can help you help your child to use these aids:

▶ Identify the title of the graphic and discuss what information is being illustrated.

▶ When working with a graph, start by identifying what kind it is: pie graph, line graph, bar graph, or pictograph. Examples of each are shown on page 101.

▶ Read line graphs, bar graphs, pictographs, tables, and charts from the "outside in." In other words, look first at any headings at the top, the bottom, and along both sides before moving to the information contained in the graphic.

▶ When working with a graph or a timeline, identify the unit of measure used. *Examples:* inch, foot, or mile; day, week, month, or year; quantity; etc.

▶ When working with a diagram, determine how it is labeled. *Example:* A skeleton may have labels for each bone.

▶ Determine the meanings of any symbols on the graphic.

▶ Discuss ways in which the graphic can be used. *Examples:* A graphic of toy sales before and after Christmas can help store owners decide how many toys to stock up on each month and how many cash registers to keep open. An airplane schedule is a table used by airport employees, passengers, and persons taking passengers to or from the airport.

▶ Take turns with your child inventing questions that can be answered by studying the graphic.

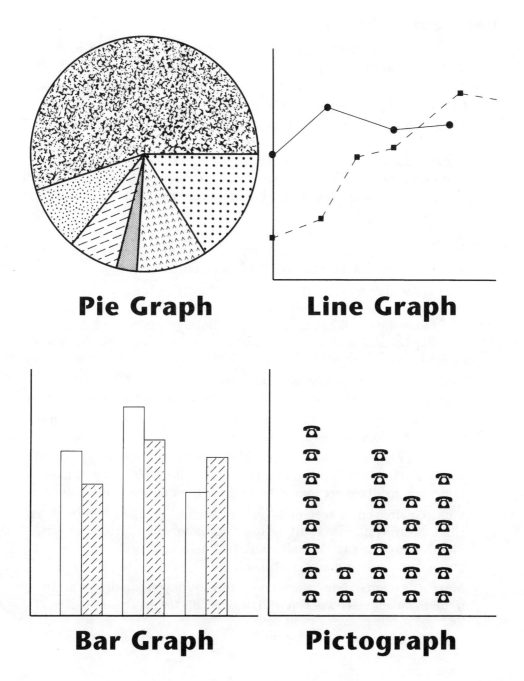

Pie Graph

Line Graph

Bar Graph

Pictograph

Making graphics fun

▸ Play games that stress geography and graphic skills mastery. See Chapter 9 for suggestions.

▸ Develop "graphics radar." Both you and your child can keep an eye out for graphics, then discuss them together. The national newspaper, *USA Today*, is an excellent resource for clear, colorful maps, charts, and graphs of all kinds.

▸ If your child is a sports fan, keep a map handy so he can locate the home cities of favorite teams. When watching sports events, use a map or globe to locate the countries, cities, and continents mentioned during the competition.

▸ If your child is an animal fancier, locate the countries and continents that are the original homes of his favorite animals. On trips to the zoo, take a small world map along for the same purpose.

▸ When planning a family trip, help your child to locate your destination on a map. If you'll be traveling by plane, discuss how long it would take to get there by car. When touring a city, locate points of interest on a city map (available from most Boards of Tourism or Information offices or kiosks).

▸ Send away for a map of your child's favorite amusement or theme park. Learning map reading skills is fun when the map is colorful and exciting.

▸ Purchase a large, colorful floor or wall map of the world and place it in your child's room or study center.

▸ Most shopping malls provide centrally located maps of their stores and shops. The next time you go shopping with your child, lead him to one of these maps. Then let your child lead *you* from one store to another.

▸ Many children enjoy keeping behavior charts on a daily basis. Let your child construct his own chart for tracking chores done, homework completed, numbers of books read, math facts mastered, and so on. Record progress with check marks or stickers.

▸ Make a "pedigree chart" showing the lineage of your family, or make a family timeline. (These can also be nice gifts for relatives.)

 **HELP!**

"My son is in the fifth grade. His next science test is going to be on the human skeletal system. His teacher will give him a diagram of the skeleton, and he'll have to label the bones. How can I help him prepare?"

Make multiple photocopies of a *clear* picture or drawing of a skeleton and have your son practice writing in the correct name for each bone. It may take many repetitions before he knows them all (which is the reason behind the need for multiple photocopies), so be patient and encouraging. If you can come up with any mnemonics or "memory tricks" (for example, "Elvis the pelvis"), so much the better.

"My daughter got a D on her last social studies test. She told me that she had read the chapter carefully and didn't understand why her grade was so low. We looked over the questions she missed and discovered that the information she needed to know was in the chapter, but it was presented in charts and timelines rather than the text. My daughter claims that she 'skipped those parts' because she didn't think they were important."

This isn't at all uncommon. Many children perceive graphics as "free spaces" in reading and simply advance to the next paragraph. Communicate to your daughter the importance of graphic information, using the suggestions given on pages 98–102.

"My son never has trouble reading graphs, diagrams, or maps of any kind. How can I encourage him to develop this talent further?"

Why not name him the "Official Navigator" on family vacations? This will give him the opportunity to put his skills to work in real-life situations. Allow him plenty of time in advance to study the maps you'll be using; if he's responsible for reading them under pressure or during times of peak traffic, or if he makes an error and you take a wrong turn, you'll both get frustrated.

You can also encourage your son to include graphics in his school reports and projects. Creating graphics may be time-consuming (especially without the aid of computer graphics software), but they add that "something extra" that children enjoy—and teachers often reward.

"My daughter doesn't like science and thinks it's really for boys. What can I do to encourage her to get interested in science?"

Expose her to the world of female scientists. One resource you can start with is *Girls and Young Women Inventing: 20 True Stories about Inventors Plus How You Can Be One Yourself* by Frances A. Karnes and Suzanne M. Bean (Minneapolis: Free Spirit Publishing, 1995). You can also lead your daughter to biographies of women who have made their mark in science. Following is a starter list to use as you search the library (or the Internet) for information. For more ideas, see *Women's World: A Timeline of Women in History* by Irene M. Franck and David M. Brownstone (New York: HarperCollins, 1995).

- Anthropologist Margaret Mead
- Anthropologist Mary Douglas Leakey
- Astronaut Judith Resnik
- Astronaut Sally Ride
- Astronomer Margaret Burbidge
- Aviator and sailor Marion Rice Hart
- Chemist Rachel Fuller Brown
- Civil engineer Elsie Eaves
- Computer scientist Grace Brewster Murray Hopper
- Conservationist Joy Gessner Adamson
- Cosmonaut Valentina Tereshkova
- Geneticist Barbara McClintock
- Geologist Doris Malkin Curtis
- Microbiologist Alice Evans
- Nobel Prize winner Gertrude Elion
- Nuclear physicist Rosalyn Yalow
- Nutritionist Adele Davis
- Physician (and U.S. Surgeon General) Joycelyn Elders
- Physician Myra Adele Logan
- Physicist Mary Beth Stearns
- Primatologist Dian Fossey

How to help your child with thematic units

Thematic units are a multidisciplinary route to learning. Teachers who use thematic units spend a great deal of time planning their academic subjects around a theme such as space, insects, or electricity. Although this planning is quite a challenge, teachers need to make certain that all district-level curriculum objectives are included during the year. And many teachers who use thematic units think that the time and effort are worth it. Students benefit because their learning is connected, meaningful, memorable, and exciting.

Some thematic units—such as those on gun safety or cultural heritage—are taught schoolwide or districtwide.

Writing expert Lucy Calkins and her colleagues like to tell parents, "Your child's reading, writing, and theme studies will spill over into your home this year. . . and we want their obsessions and passions and projects to spill over from the home into the classroom as well." They hope and expect that children will consciously and deliberately weave literacy together with the passions, projects, and people of their lives. A good way to help this happen is by getting involved with theme studies in your child's classroom. You might provide resources for the teacher to use, or you might find ways to extend one or more themes into your family activities. Ask the teacher for a list of themes your child's class will be exploring, along with a schedule of when they will be featured during the year. Then tailor the suggestions on pages 106–107 to fit the thematic unit your child is currently experiencing.

 **HELP!**

"The science and social studies program at my daughter's school is confusing to me. I hear about weekly lessons on tree planting and drug awareness, but I'm concerned that I hear nothing about geography or history."

Most districts will have a comprehensive scope-and-sequence plan for science and social studies into which these units can be integrated. Ask about the curriculum at your school and how your child's teacher is planning to cover the instructional objectives.

12 ways to build your child's fund of general information

Children who have a rich fund of general information and background knowledge on a variety of subjects will find science and social studies (and reading and writing) easier and more interesting than those who don't. As a caring parent, you have the privilege and the responsibility of sharing the world with your child.

Describe your own childhood experiences, the things that interested you then (and interest you now), your favorite places, and whatever else occurs to you. Be ready at a moment's notice to answer questions that occur to your child—or promise to help her find the answers if you don't know them yourself. Talk, talk, talk—about feelings, hobbies, politics, advertisements, TV shows, music, roller skates, road signs, poems, movies, grandparents, pets, anything and everything! And listen, listen, listen to your child.

A child who's treated as someone worth talking to develops a sense of value and self-respect. A child who's treated as someone worth listening to develops strong verbal skills and an undying curiosity. And both of you together develop better communication and a deeper understanding of each other's wants and needs, hopes and dreams, personalities and beings. The more you converse with each other, the more rewarding your conversations and your relationship will become.

Here are suggestions for stimulating activities to enjoy with your child. Talk about them before; talk about them during; talk about them after!

1. Check public radio and television listings for news, documentaries, and other interesting programs, then listen and watch together.

2. If you have an encyclopedia on CD-ROM, explore it with your child. If you have an Internet connection, consider subscribing to Encyclopedia Britannica Online. For more information, visit the Web site: http://www.eb.com/

3. If you have access to the Internet, explore various Web sites with your child, such as those listed on page 131.

4. When renting or buying videos for home viewing, include educational tapes.

5. Take your child to natural history museums, science museums, art museums, children's museums, zoos, botanical gardens, historical sites, and more.

6. Take your child to national parks and forests and go on tours with the rangers.

7. Have your child read articles in a newspaper or in news magazines, or read them aloud to her.

8. Take *frequent* trips to the public library. (Jim Trelease, the author of *The New Read-Aloud Handbook*, asks parents to think about their priorities by comparing the number of times they take their kids to the library vs. the number of times they take them to the shopping mall.) If your child is mature enough and has developed library skills, you can go to the library together and arrange to meet in a certain place at a certain time (an hour later, for example). Then let her have the run of the place. One child we know was eagerly scanning microfiche when he was still too short to reach

it without standing on a chair. And he knew from an early age how to ask librarians for directions and suggestions. His idea of a "fun night out" was an evening spent at the library!

9. Make vacations learning experiences. Read travel guides together and let your child participate in the where-to-go, what-to-see decision-making process.

10. Watch *quality* movies with your child, then discuss them afterward. Don't just limit your choices to commercial theaters. Check out movies offered at libraries, museums, and other cultural centers. And don't restrict your choices to current movies. If you have a VCR, use it to screen old comedies, historical dramas, and adventures.

11. Plan "theme" birthday parties with your child that involve some research. *Examples:* An American Revolution costume party; an Inventor's Convention; a play.

12. Take advantage of every "teachable moment" that presents itself during the course of a normal day: trips to the grocery store, gardening, walks around the block, meal preparation, dinnertime discussions, and many, many more.

Remember: Your child is eager to learn. *And you are your child's most important teacher.*

 **HELP!**

"There are books in our local bookstore about everything my child should know in each grade. Should I buy these books and drill my child on this material?"

Research has shown that information learned in small, isolated bits is quickly forgotten. Rather than investing your time (and money) on books like these, expose your child to an ever-increasing fund of information, as described on pages 105–107.

How to help your child with foreign languages

In elementary school, foreign languages have traditionally been taught for enrichment. As countries become more multicultural and the world becomes more interdependent, the need to speak more than one language is increasing. In most elementary schools, the foreign language teacher is a specialist who visits the elementary classroom once, twice, or more often during the week. The curriculum varies greatly. If your child is given the opportunity to receive foreign language instruction, start by finding out about the program. Ask questions like these:

- ▶ "How often will the class meet?"
- ▶ "How intensive will the instruction be?"
- ▶ "What kinds of things will my child be learning?"
- ▶ "Will homework be required? If so, what can I do to help at home?"

Like one's native language, a foreign language is learned more by practice and "absorption" than by any conscious effort to master the rules of grammar. (In any event, these come later, not in the elementary curriculum.) Your child's practice can be aided by television, videocassettes, audiocassettes, records, foreign language clubs, and pen pals. Naturally, the preferred way to learn a language is to live in a country where it is spoken, but this is not an option for most young children. If you're planning a foreign vacation anyway, you may want to consider visiting a country where your child can hear the language he is studying. You might also explore exchange student programs. If your school doesn't keep a file of exchange program addresses, contact the embassy of a country whose people speak the language you're interested in.

An important point to remember when helping your child with a foreign language is *not to overcorrect*. Children who are learning English are allowed to experiment—for example, with "ed" as the past tense form of all verbs, including "runned." Children who are learning a foreign language should be given the same leeway.

Making language learning fun

Learning about other cultures can be fascinating. Here are several suggestions to try with your child:

- ▶ Read to your child about life in the country (or countries) where people speak the language he's learning.
- ▶ If you have friends from that country (or countries), ask them if they are willing to spend some time talking with your child.
- ▶ Seek out articles in *National Geographic* and travel magazines (the more pictures, the better).

- ▸ Volunteer to assist with International Fairs at your child's school.

- ▸ Obtain posters and other small items from travel agents or import shops.

- ▸ Visit a local restaurant that specializes in foods of the country.

- ▸ Talk to friends around the world on the Internet.

- ▸ Try using games, especially if you can speak the language. Work with your child to make flash cards of the words your child is learning. Since most of these will have to do with animals, foods, colors, people, and actions, make word-and-picture cards for playing Concentration (see pages 141–142) or Wet Cat (a game similar to Old Maid). Make cards to teach vocabulary from the language and facts about the countries where it is spoken, then use a trivia board game to track progress and keep score.

- ▸ Use your imagination!

 **HELP!**

"My daughter is a good student and is taking Spanish in school. However, she isn't at all motivated to practice the phrases she's assigned for homework."

Talk with the teacher to determine the reason for your daughter's "couldn't care less" attitude. She may be afraid to take risks, which studying a foreign language certainly demands. She may be hesitant to pronounce the new words for fear of being ridiculed. Or she may be finding that foreign languages don't come as easily to her as other subjects.

Start by relaxing any demands you are currently making on her to "do well" in her Spanish class. Instead, emphasize the value and fun of learning a new language. Make an effort to learn the words she is being taught so the two of you can have mini-conversations. She may feel more encouraged to take risks if you demonstrate that *you* are.

If these approaches are unsuccessful, it may be wise to let your daughter discontinue her Spanish instruction until she is older and perhaps more interested. Although some aspects of language learning are easier when one is very young, this is not true for all aspects. Plus learning is easier when motivation is higher. Instead of spoiling any desire your daughter might have to learn a foreign language in the future, let it go for now.

"My son has difficulty reading in English, and now he's also being taught to read in French. Will this cause a problem?"

Knowledge of two languages generally promotes conceptual development in both, and this development is directly related to reading skills. So studying French shouldn't hurt your son. However, if he continues to have a hard time reading English, he should take a second language only if the emphasis is on speaking rather than reading.

"My son is excited about learning French and is picking up oral French easily. But he has problems reading in French, and this problem prevents him from completing his homework."

Your son is mastering the most difficult aspect of the new language, for which he should be praised and encouraged. You might want to find out whether his teacher or an advanced student could record his homework on audiocassette so he can read and listen simultaneously. Some of the suggestions for improving reading skills found in Chapter 3 might also be helpful here.

"My daughter does well on her weekly Spanish quizzes, but she has difficulty with tests that cover several units. It seems that while she's learning the material in one unit, she's forgetting everything she learned before."

Your daughter needs to review previous lessons on a regular basis. Learning a foreign language is a cumulative process; you can't just learn the new and "dump" the old. You can help her to review by adapting the suggestions found on pages 96–98.

"My son studies with a friend every evening. They practice their Spanish together, but neither uses a very good Spanish accent. Should I let them continue?"

Be glad that your son is practicing and progressing without your overt assistance. The only help you should offer is to provide videocassettes, audiocassettes, or records to expand their practice. In time, their accents should improve.

7

How to Help Your Child with Formal Assessments, Projects, Reports, and Papers

"I make them believe in themselves."

Jaime Escalante

How to help your child prepare for formal assessment

Over your child's school career, he or she may participate in formal assessment a number of times. Most often, this will be in the form of standardized tests of reading and math, such as the Stanford Achievement Test (SAT), the Comprehensive Test of Basic Skills (CTBS), or the Iowa Test of Basic Skills (ITBS), and perhaps also tests of writing to a prompt. Following are tips to help you prepare your child for these important events.

Standardized tests of reading and math

Preparation for standardized reading and math tests is an ongoing process. Children who read a lot and are read to regularly, who think through problems, and who have good attention spans are more likely to do better on standardized tests than other children. In addition to the ongoing preparation inherent in the suggestions throughout this book, you can help your child in the following ways:

- ▸ If homework involves multiple choice answers, have your child explain why one answer is correct *and* why the others are incorrect.
- ▸ When your child practices math facts, be sure that she writes them both horizontally and vertically.
- ▸ When your child is reading (or you're reading to your child), have her tell you the main idea or what the story or selection is mostly about.
- ▸ Expose your child to new vocabulary. Use interesting words when you talk to her, and read aloud from books that introduce new words.
- ▸ Take turns with your child asking and answering questions about material which has been read, allowing for "lookbacks" to find the answers.

You might also use homework which involves multiple-choice answers as test-taking practice. Here's how:

1. Read each possible answer *with* the stem. This helps your child focus on the right answer to the given question. *Example:* For this question. . .

   Many children like:

   A. pizza

   B. hamburgers

   C. ice cream

   D. all of the above.

   . . . you would say, "Many children like pizza. Many children like hamburgers. Many children like ice cream. Many children like all of the above."

2. Model reading *all* choices before choosing an answer, explaining out loud why each choice seems to be right or wrong. *Example:* "'Many children like pizza.' That's true, so maybe that's the right answer. But let's try the next ones to make sure they aren't the right answers. 'Many children like hamburgers.' 'Many children like ice cream.' Those are true, too! This may be a tough one! Let's see. The last choice is, 'Many children like all of the above.' Ah, that's the right answer!"

3. Show your child how to use the process of elimination. *Example:* "If B, C, and D are definitely wrong, then the answer must be A."

Writing to a prompt

Your child may receive formal writing assessment beginning in the intermediate grades. With such assessment, children may write to a given prompt. (*Examples:* "Pretend you woke up one morning and found yourself to be two inches tall. Tell about your day." "Explain how to make a peanut butter sandwich.") The "score" for such an assessment—often a number from 1 to 6—will combine all areas of writing, from content to spelling and grammar.

The best preparation for this type of assessment is time for daily writing, frequent conversations about writing strengths and possibilities for improvement, and time for revision. Aside from the suggestions given in Chapter 4, you can help your child with formal writing assessment by working with composition homework as follows:

- ▶ Ask the teacher if there is a rubric or scoring system you can have so you can see what areas of writing are assessed in your child's classroom.

- ▶ On a regular basis, celebrate fine turns of phrase in material read by you or your child. This provides excellent modeling.

- ▶ Use a highlighter to note any exceptional word choices your child makes in her writing (*example:* "lion-hearted" instead of "brave").

- ▶ Let your child write on a computer, if one is available. If not, have her write on every other line of the paper to allow for easy revision.

- ▶ When your child is given a topic to write about, help her to stay on the topic.

- ▶ Help to ensure that your child's final drafts are organized from beginning to end.

- ▶ Help to ensure that your child adds supporting details for her ideas.

- ▶ Once the above areas are addressed, focus on spellings of commonly misspelled words (e.g., *because, a lot, too, their*) and on basic punctuation and grammar.

CAUTION

Children's tolerance for revision varies. If your child's tolerance is minimal, go only as far as you can with these suggestions without causing undue discomfort to your child (and to you).

Conquering test anxiety

You might think of test anxiety as a bell-shaped curve. At one end are test-takers who are too anxious and don't do well; at the other are test-takers who couldn't care less about how they perform. A moderate degree of anxiety will produce the best results. To encourage an appropriate amount of test anxiety in your child (and discourage panic or indifference), try these suggestions:

1. Occasionally have your child complete her homework with a timer and without any help so she becomes accustomed to working under test-like conditions.

2. Teach your child to take brief "relaxation breaks" if she starts getting too anxious. *Example:* "Close your eyes. Breathe deeply. Think about tensing, then relaxing every part of your body, from your toes to the top of your head."

3. Consider taking your child out for a special breakfast on the day of an important test. We know of one parent who did this for her child's first standardized test so the child would have positive associations with testing.

How to help your child with special projects

Art Fair, Science Fair, social studies displays! Special projects are a welcome diversion from daily ditto sheets and textbook assignments—but they can also be a nightmare for parents. If your child doesn't quite know what to do or how to do it, *you* could end up bearing the burden.

There is a way to achieve more child participation and less parental involvement, and it's called *planning.* As soon as the assignment is made, you and your child should meet to discuss it and plot out a project plan. The following list of steps can get you started. A checklist you can copy and use is found on pages 174–175.

1. Decide on the project theme.

2. Have the theme approved by the teacher.

3. Make a list of things that need to be done and the order in which they should be completed.

4. Decide who is going to do what.

5. Set deadlines for completing each part of the project.

6. Make a list of the materials needed.

7. Make a projected budget.

8. Send away for resource materials needed.

9. Contact community resources.

10. Visit the library.

11. Complete the project on schedule.

Special projects can be fun, *if* children are allowed to choose themes that interest them and *if* they are encouraged (not smothered) by parental supervision. As you work with your child, lend your support when it is needed and when it is asked for. Avoid the temptation to do the project for your child. (We shouldn't hear parents ask each other, "What did *you* get on the science fair project?") Great joy can be found in a job well done—and independently done.

If you have Internet access, this can add a new and exciting dimension to special projects. The World Wide Web is a wealth of information on any topic you can imagine. You and your child might start by exploring the sites listed on page 131. Ask the teacher and your school or district media specialist for more recommendations.

 **HELP!**

"My daughter doesn't have any ideas for her science fair experiment. I have no clue about what's appropriate and what isn't. Where can we go to get ideas?"

Look around you. You may find inspiration in the kitchen for experiments on heat, refrigeration, or decay. You may find inspiration in the garden for experiments on plant or insect development. For additional ideas, talk to a librarian— or a friendly scientist in your community. Or turn to one of these resources:

▶ *Great Science Fair Projects* by Phyllis Katz and Janet Frekko (New York: Franklin Watts, 1992).

▶ *100 Amazing Make-It-Yourself Science Fair Projects* by Glen Vecchione (New York: Sterling Publishing Co., 1995).

"Last year my son was supposed to make a social studies display, but I did all the work. I refuse to do it again this year. What can I do to get him involved?"

Follow the steps on pages 114–115. Decide first what needs to be done, then who is going to do it. Because you're trying to limit your involvement, confine your contributions to tasks like providing transportation to the library, proofreading a first draft, or supplying opportunities for your son to earn money to cover the cost of the project. See page 176 for a form the two of you can use to make your arrangement "official."

"My son simply can't draw. Last year his social studies poster was a disaster! Should I do it for him this year?"

If your son is truly embarrassed by his inability to draw, perhaps his teacher can suggest another format for the poster. For example, if you have access to a computer graphics program (and it's one your son can learn to use), this may be the solution.

"Last year at our school, the Science Fair mostly consisted of *parent* projects. My daughter completed her project all by herself, and it was obviously not as polished as the others. Should I help her more this year?"

Independence is the primary goal of any special project. If your daughter is content to complete her project on her own, more power to her. Be available to serve as a resource, but continue to foster her independent spirit. In other words, hands off!

How to help your child with book reports

With the threat of illiteracy looming all about us, teachers are encouraging students to read, read, and read some more. It isn't unusual for elementary school children to be required to complete a book each week or (in upper grades) a longer, more substantial book each month. As a caring parent, you can support this excellent emphasis on reading by taking regular trips to the library or bookstore with your child, and by planning regular family reading times. Given the choice, most children will opt to rent the video or audiocassette over reading the book. Don't give the choice. Insist that multimedia aids be used as supplements rather than substitutes for the real thing.

In many classrooms today, the formal book report is a thing of the past. Instead, children are required to complete alternate assignments to give evidence of having read a book. Posters, puppets, and plays have supplanted written reports, with some teachers devising a variety of creative options. Many teachers who still assign book reports provide a format for children to follow. If your child is assigned a book report, and if the teacher doesn't provide a format, the outlines on pages 177–188 can serve as frameworks for writing reports on three different kinds of books: fiction, nonfiction, and biography.

A book report is generally perceived as something to slog through. (You probably don't have especially fond memories from your own childhood where book reports are concerned.) They may not be the most fascinating and stimulating of all assignments, but they do serve several purposes. They get children reading, and they get them reading *carefully*. If children know that they're going to have to write about something they read, they're less likely to skim it. A good book report format also trains a child to pay attention to details like setting, characters, and plot.

The most critical factor in making a book report more bearable is finding a proper match between a book and a child. Help your child select a book that is both interesting and readable. Ask your school or public librarian for suggestions. Find out if the teacher has a list of recommended books that are likely to appeal to your child. If your child is assigned a book and is not given the luxury of choosing, help him plan enough time to complete it. Work reading assignments into his homework schedule or incorporate them into your family reading time.

 **HELP!**

"My son is required to hand in a book report every other week. It's a constant hassle at our house. The night before the report is due, we're always pushing him to get it done. Isn't this too severe an assignment for a fifth grader?"

If the book report is always being done the night before it's due, then it *is* "too severe" an assignment—for you and your family. Help your son select books that are interesting to him and are written at a comfortable level of difficulty. Then help him establish a reading schedule that enables him to complete his reading early. Two nights before the report is due, encourage him to write a rough draft. Work with him to proofread it and find and correct any errors. The night before the report is due, he can complete the final draft—a much easier and more manageable task than starting cold.

"My daughter is assigned a book a month. She is required to read the book and then take an in-class test based on her reading. She has failed every test. This month the assigned book is *Johnny Tremain*. She claims that she can't understand the book and wants to rent the video instead."

If the book is extremely difficult for your daughter to read, viewing the video may enable her to grasp the basic story line. *Watch it with her* well in advance of when the test is scheduled. Then encourage her to read one chapter of the book at a time and discuss it with you. Use the book report outlines on pages 177–180 to help her study for the test.

"My daughter loves to read but hates to write book reports. She'll talk about a book forever, but writing a report is sheer torture. How can I help make this task more tolerable for her?"

Use the outlines on pages 177–188 to provide structure. Following a format greatly simplifies report writing. If your daughter likes to talk about a book she has just read, encourage her to talk into a recorder while following one of the outlines. When she finishes, she can transcribe her oral report into written form.

"My son would rather read than eat. He reads many more books than required by his teacher, and he writes well-developed book reports. Should I be concerned about his preoccupation with reading?"

Only if he is using reading as a substitute for real-life activities or relationships. If his life is balanced—if he also participates in school activities, plays with friends, and pursues non-book interests—then celebrate the fact that he has formed such a good habit at such a young age.

How to help your child with term papers

Helping your child with a written report may bring flashbacks of your own late nights spent hunched over a typewriter in a dormitory room. Grinding out a report at the last minute is nobody's idea of fun. Fortunately, your child can learn from you the benefits of advance planning.

Often children are assigned a report without receiving any instruction on how to go about doing it. Or they may not be taught how to use instruction given previously. For example, children may learn how to outline in a language arts class, but may not be shown how to apply this skill to a term paper for a social studies class. Even if they are told what to do, they may never have seen a sample of a finished report. In other words, they may have no idea what is expected of them!

Planning is the key to a successful paper-writing experience. You may have gotten by on all-nighters, but it's your duty as a caring parent to help your child develop healthier habits. With patience and guidance from you, she can learn to live with a far more organized and efficient schedule. The following list of steps can get you started. A checklist you can copy and use is found on pages 189–190.

1. Make sure that your child understands the assignment.
2. Find out all the requirements and specifications for the paper. *Examples:* Will it need a title page? A table of contents? A bibliography? Pictures, illustrations, maps, or other graphics? Should it be typed or word processed, or can it be handwritten?
3. Decide on a topic.
4. Have the topic approved by the teacher.
5. Research the topic at the library and/or use home technology resources (CD-ROM encyclopedia, Internet resources, etc.).
6. Contact community resources related to the topic.
7. Write letters needed to obtain information from national sources.
8. Take notes on the materials found or obtained.
9. Develop an outline.
10. Write a rough draft.
11. Proofread the rough draft using the A-OK method (see pages 72–73).
12. Write the final draft.

Work with your child to set a deadline for each step of this checklist. Decide what she can do independently and where you will need to help. Our experience has shown that the most difficult steps are note-taking, outlining, and writing the rough draft. A child about to do her first report will probably need a great deal of guidance and support during these steps.

 **HELP!**

"My daughter, a fourth grader, has been assigned a term paper on Norway. She did a report on volleyball last month and got a C. Her teacher was upset that she copied from the encyclopedia. My daughter has no idea how to write a report."

"My son prints out pages he downloads from the Internet and turns these in as term papers. He doesn't understand that this isn't acceptable."

When teachers require children to write reports without giving them any formal instruction, parental assistance is much needed. Never write a report *for* your child, but do help your child to extract information from varied resources and reference materials (including printed materials—books, magazines—and those available through technology resources including CD-ROMs and the

Internet) and put this information into his or her own words. Give your child a copy of the checklist on pages 189–190 to serve as a guide in planning the project.

Try to make this a positive experience in any way you can. For a daughter assigned a term paper on Norway, you might ask a travel agent for pictures or write to various sources (*example:* the Norwegian Embassy) for information. For a son who loves to surf the Internet, you might encourage him to find several papers or resources on his topic and pull information from all of them into his final report. Or he might post a query in a news group and see what responses come in. (One student we know gathered responses from top scientists around the world.) Your child will be writing reports for a long time, so anything you can do to instill a positive attitude will be extremely important.

"Last year my son wrote a term paper for school. He did a good job, but he waited until the night before to do most of the work. How can I help him budget his time better?"

Guide him through the steps on page 119, assigning dates and deadlines to each step. Give him a copy of the checklist on pages 189–190 to use for his own reference. Work out a system of rewards for successful completion of each step.

"My son enjoys research and does a fine job of writing term papers for school. What can I do to let him know that I support his efforts—without interfering?"

When your son is researching a topic, communicate to him that you are interested in what he is doing. Let him share his findings at the dinner table. Keep your eyes and ears open for community resources which may enhance his research.

Using Technology

*"We should be thrilled that so much technology is available,
and we should use whatever we can get our hands on. . . .
Don't worry about students becoming dependent on technology.
Just be glad it's available to make learning
more accessible and exciting for everyone."*

Susan Winebrenner

Homework and home computers

Many parents have asked us whether it's a good idea for their children to use a computer when doing homework. Our answer is: It depends. Clearly it's important for children to be comfortable around computers and to know what computers can do—in short, to become computer literate. Making a computer available in the home is an excellent way to facilitate this. But be prepared to exercise some parental control! Excessive use of computers is as bad as too much TV. Children who are always in front of computer monitors don't have time for socializing, reading, or exercise.

If you already own a computer, consider letting your child use it at appropriate times but not constantly, and provide software that encourages him to study and learn. There are many programs available today that can enliven repetitive drill-and-practice in math, reading, and spelling. They won't necessarily help with Tuesday night's specific homework assignments, but they may sharpen your child's skills in the required areas. And that's a benefit for the long term.

What if you don't already own a home computer? Should you consider buying one? If you can afford one, it would be a good investment, especially if

121

your child is using computers in school. You may opt to purchase a computer that's identical to or compatible with the kind the school has chosen. Check with your child's teacher or the school media center or technology center specialist for specifics.

If a computer isn't in your budget. . .

A home computer may not be in your family budget at the present time. However, there are some steps you can take to make sure that your child has the opportunity to explore the world of computers.

- ▶ Some schools have programs that allow parents to borrow a computer for as long as a month at a time. If your school doesn't have such a program, work with the parents' organization to create one.
- ▶ Office support centers such as Kinko's have computers available for customers to "rent" on site. While this might prove expensive over time, it may help you to explore word processing systems and decide if a computer is something worth planning and saving for.
- ▶ Ask about opportunities at your child's school; perhaps computers in the media or technology center can be used before or after school. Learn what your child is learning with respect to word processing, programming, and use of software programs.
- ▶ See if your library offers computer use time.

How to decide what software to buy

Computer software can be expensive, the boxes seldom tell you much about the programs inside, and clerks aren't always helpful. Heeding cries for help, some software distributors and buying clubs allow customers to "try before they buy" and offer money-back guarantees. Here are two distributors you can contact:

- ▶ BrightIdeas, 1 Jacob Way, Reading, MA 01867; telephone (617) 942-3075. Has consultants on staff to help match software to customers; offers a 30-day money-back guarantee. On the WWW: http://www.awl.com/www.brightideas.com/
- ▶ KidSoft, 10275 De Anza, Cupertino, CA 95014; toll-free telephone 1-800-354-6164. On the WWW: http://www.kidsoft.com/

Several books currently available provide detailed reviews of educational and entertainment programs. Look for these at your library or bookstore:

- *The Computer Museum Guide to the Best Software for Kids* by Cathy Miranker and Alison Elliot (New York: HarperPerennial, 1995).
- *The Family PC Software Buyer's Guide* by Kurt Carlson and Valle Dwight (New York: Hyperion, 1996).
- *Kidware: The Parent's Guide to Software for Children* by Michael Perkins and Celia Núñez (Rocklin, CA: Prima, 1995).
- *That's Edutainment! A Parent's Guide to Educational Software* by Eric Brown (New York: McGraw-Hill, 1996).

Other suggestions:

- Your school or local public library might have software you can check out and sample at home.
- Some stores that specialize in computer software and hardware allow customers to try software before buying it, and also allow boxed programs to be returned within 30 days if customers aren't satisfied with them. (Department and discount stores are less likely to be as liberal with their return policies.)
- You might try previewing games at the homes of your child's friends.
- Consult publications like *Family Computing, Family PC, PC World,* and *Macworld* for previews, reviews, and letters from readers about software programs.

Recommended criteria for choosing software

The best software programs aren't necessarily those with the most awesome technology. Rather, the best programs are those that enhance your child's strengths and interests, just as good books or videos can do. Cathy Miranker, coauthor of *The Computer Museum Guide to the Best Software for Kids,* says that software should satisfy the "three L's": *learning, looks,* and *longevity.* Aside from issues of educational soundness (which is sometimes hard for parents to evaluate), smooth functioning, and affordability, the following criteria should help you to decide what software to buy.

Brand name

Chances are better than average with publishers with proven track records such as Davidson & Associates, Edmark, Broderbund, and Maxis. Avoid deeply discounted software, which usually means that the programs have done poorly in the marketplace.

Compatibility with home equipment

Jot down your computer's specs (brand, PC or Macintosh, model, RAM, hard drive size, etc.) and carry them with you when shopping. Does a new program require a joystick, more memory, or some other add-on? If so, would it be worth making this purchase for use with additional programs as well?

Ease of use

How long will it take for your child to learn the program? Is her reading level adequate for the program? Can she quit the program for a while and return quickly to where she left off earlier?

Interest level

Are the audio and visual presentations appealing? Is the program likely to be enjoyable for your child? Does it move speedily enough to hold her interest?

Variety

Is there enough variety in the program that your child will want to return to it again and again?

21st century awareness

Does the software promote the skills important for 21st century learners, such as independent thinking, critical thinking, and investigative problem-solving?

Challenge

Does the program span a wide range of age and skill levels so your child can grow with it? How long will it take your child to feel a sense of accomplishment from using the program?

Child control

Will your child merely respond to prompts from the program, or will she have an opportunity to create individual pathways toward learning?

Appropriate rewards

Will your child feel that she has created or discovered something after using the software, or is the only "reward" a point value for the number of correct answers? Does feedback include clues? Is the feedback generally supportive and encouraging?

Programs that promote critical thinking and problem solving*

Some of the more creative programs on the market build critical thinking and problem solving skills, a long-term benefit. Children who learn to think will learn to draw on this ability on many different occasions. Recommended programs include:

▸ *Fatty Bear's Birthday Surprise.* Ages 9–13. A pesky puppy has run off with cake decorations and fixings. Children accompany Fatty Bear through the house, gathering clues. The program offers over 30 locations to explore, as well as age-appropriate logic puzzles. It entertains as it builds problem-solving and critical thinking skills. From Humongous Entertainment.

▸ *OutNumbered!* Ages 11–13. Children sit for hours trying to find the Master of Mischief as they solve problems in game form. From The Learning Company (SoftKey, International).

▸ The *Sim* Series. Children and adults engage in exciting simulated problems in *SimPark* and *SimTown* (ages 8–12) and *SimFarm, SimLife, SimAnt,* and *SimCity* (ages 12 and up). From Maxis.

▸ *Thinkin' Things* Collections. *Collection 1* (ages 4–8) strengthens observation, memory, and problem-solving skills while encouraging creativity. *Collection 2* (ages 6–12) strengthens observation, analysis, spatial awareness, and memory skills and fosters creativity. *Collection 3* (ages 7–13) improves deductive and inductive reasoning, synthesis and analysis skills. From Edmark.

▸ *Where in the World Is Carmen SanDiego?* This old favorite for ages 10 and up continues to motivate interest in geography and other cultures. A deluxe edition is enhanced with spectacular sounds and graphics. Other programs in the series (*Where in Space. . .* for ages 11 and up, *Where in the USA. . .* for ages 10 and up) are equally good. From Broderbund.

Programs that teach keyboarding

Before a child can successfully use a word processor, he must first learn how to type, or "keyboard." Keyboarding should be taught as soon as children have to enter more than single characters (Y, N, numbers) into the keyboard. Some inexpensive programs that teach keyboarding include:

---

* Addresses, telephone numbers, and Web site addresses for the software publishers named in this and the following sections are found on pages 128–129.

- *Ultrakey.* Ages 8–17. The strengths of this 13-unit program lie in its graphics and flexibility. Each lesson supplies information about correct fingering and gives students an opportunity to practice. From Bytes of Learning.

- *Kid Works 2.* Ages 9–13. This early typing and writing program uses large letters on "lined paper." From Davidson & Associates.

- *Mario Teaches Typing.* Ages 9–13. Mario, the Nintendo character, teaches children to type in this inexpensive high-action program, an entertaining extension of a more formal keyboarding curriculum. From Interplay Productions.

- *Mavis Beacon Teaches Typing.* Ages 9 and up. This program "speaks" in conversational tones while analyzing typing mistakes. Users can type in jokes, riddles, and rhymes. The program also displays a keyboard with fingers that type along with the user, and a built-in metronome encourages even typing. Includes an "Indy Racer" game. From Mindscape.

Programs that teach word processing

Although all children should learn to compose with a pencil, word processing programs can greatly simplify tasks ranging from vocabulary sentences to book reports. They make it easy to insert or delete sentences, reorganize paragraphs, look up a word in a built-in thesaurus, and correct spelling and grammar. You may need to teach your child the proper use of these tools. *Example:* A spellchecker or grammar-check program may highlight words that are correct, or words that your child will have reason to leave "as is." This can be confusing and will require some explanation.

CAUTION

Check with your child's teacher *before* giving your child permission to do writing assignments on the computer. Some teachers prefer that assignments be handwritten, and younger children especially need practice in this skill. Most teachers prefer that children *not* use spellcheckers.

Older children will probably be ready for standard adult word processing programs such as *Word* or *Word Perfect.* For younger students, try:

▸ *The Writing Center.* Ages 6–10. This program helps children discover the pleasures of seeing their writing in print. From The Learning Company (SoftKey, International).

Programs that reinforce basic skills

Software may focus on reinforcing specific skills, such as spelling or computation. Or it may simultaneously reinforce several skill areas; in a creative writing program, for example, students might be called on to compose, spell, and punctuate. Following are examples of both types of software.

▸ *Arthur's Teacher Troubles.* Ages 6–10. A humorous program that interactively involves children in spelling words. From The Learning Company (SoftKey, International).

▸ *Math Ace: The Grand Prix Edition.* Ages 9 and up. This program both challenges strong students and helps struggling students with real-world problems, charts and graphs, probability, geometry, algebra, and simple math facts. From Sanctuary Woods.

▸ *Math Heads.* Ages 9–13. Students "create" videos and act as contestants as they learn pre-algebra, fractions, decimals, and percentages. From Theatrix.

▸ *Sitting on the Farm.* Ages 7–11. An entertaining musical storybook designed to enhance children's reading, vocabulary, and writing skills. Students listen to a story, read the story on their own, select single words, record themselves singing while accompanied by music from the CD, fill in blanks in a story, and write original stories. From Sanctuary Woods.

▸ *Storybook Weaver.* Ages 6–10. This program motivates children to create their own stories. From MECC (SoftKey, International).

Encyclopedias on CD-ROM

CD-ROM encyclopedias bring reference works to life by using digitized pictures, animation, and video clips. Here are several for you to consider:

▸ *My First Encyclopedia.* Ages 3–6. Fun, fascinating, and *very* easy to use, this Parent's Choice Award winner invites young children to explore ten areas of learning, with no reading required. From Knowledge Adventure, Inc.

▸ *Heinemann Children's Multimedia Encyclopedia.* Ages 6–12. Based on the 11-volume *Heinemann Children's Encyclopedia.* From Reed Technology & Information Services.

▶ *Compton's Interactive Encyclopedia.* Ages 10 and up. Starting with the 1997 edition, this multimedia encyclopedia can take users to related Web sites. A Monthly Updater provides new articles and Web links and updates existing articles. From Compton's NewMedia, Inc.

▶ *The Grolier Multimedia Encyclopedia.* Appropriate for both elementary and secondary students. Based on the 33,000-article *Academic American Encyclopedia,* updated. From Grolier Interactive, Inc.

▶ *Microsoft Encarta Encyclopedia.* Ages 11 and up. A general family reference and research tool for middle school children. A Yearbook Builder feature allows users to download article updates and Month in Review summaries from the Web. From Microsoft.

Publishers of Recommended Software

▶ **Broderbund Software**, 500 Redwood Boulevard, Novato, CA 94948; for a free catalog, call toll-free 1-800-521-6263.
On the WWW: http://www.broderbund.com/

▶ **Bytes of Learning Incorporated,**150 Consumers Road, Suite 203, Willowdale, Ontario, Canada M2J 1P9; telephone (416) 495-9913; toll-free telephone 1-800-465-6428.
On the WWW: http://www.bytesoflearning.com/

▶ **Compton's NewMedia, Inc.** See SoftKey, International.
On the WWW: http://www.comptons.com/

▶ **Davidson & Associates**, 19840 Pioneer Avenue, Torrance, CA 90503; toll-free telephone 1-800-545-7677.
On the WWW: http://www.davd.com/index.html

▶ **Edmark Corporation**, P.O. Box 97021, Redmond, WA 98073-9721; toll-free telephone 1-800-426-0856.
On the WWW: http://www.edmark.com/

▶ **Grolier Interactive, Inc.**, 90 Sherman Turnpike, Danbury, CT 06816; toll-free telephone 1-800-336-3686.
On the WWW: http://www.grolier.com/

▶ **Humongous Entertainment**, 16932 Wood Red Road NE, Suite 104, Woodinville, WA 98072; toll-free telephone 1-800-499-8386.
On the WWW: http://www.humongous.com/

- **Interplay Productions**, 16815 Von Karman Avenue, Irvine, CA 92606; telephone (714) 553-6678; toll-free telephone 1-800-969-4263. On the WWW: http://www.interplay.com/

- **Knowledge Adventure, Inc.**, 1311 Grand Central Avenue, Glendale CA 91201; toll-free telephone 1-800-542-4240. On the WWW: http://www.adventure.com/

- **The Learning Company**. See SoftKey, International. On the WWW: http://www.learningco.com/

- **Maxis Software**, 2121 North California Boulevard, Suite 600, Walnut Creek, CA 94596; toll-free telephone 1-800-556-2947. On the WWW: http://www.maxis.com/

- **MECC**. See SoftKey, International. On the WWW: http://www.mecc.com/

- **Microsoft Corporation**, One Microsoft Way, Redmond, WA 98052-6399; toll-free telephone 1-800-426-9400. On the WWW: http://www.microsoft.com/

- **Mindscape**, 88 Rowland Way, Novato, CA 94945; toll-free telephone 1-800-234-3088. On the WWW: http://www.mindscape.com/

- **Reed Technology & Information Services**, 475 Virginia Drive, Ft. Washington, PA 19034; toll-free telephone 1-800-872-2828. On the WWW: http://www.rtis-c.com/

- **Sanctuary Woods**, 1825 South Grant Street, San Mateo, CA 94402; toll-free telephone 1-800-872-3518. On the WWW: http://www.sanctuary.com/

- **SoftKey, International**, One Athenaeum Street, Cambridge, MA 02142; toll-free telephone 1-800-227-5609. On the WWW: http://www.softkey.com/

- **Theatrix Interactive, Inc.**, 1250 45th Street, Suite 150, Emeryville, CA 94608-2924; toll-free telephone 1-800-955-8749. On the WWW: http://www.theatrix.com/

For comprehensive lists of Web sites and links to companies that manufacture and/or distribute educational software, try one or more of these Web addresses:

http://www.yahoo.com/Business_and_Economy/Companies/Computers/Software/Educational/

http://www.pepsite.com/Software/Publishers/H.html

Telecommunications

Telecommunications has become a communications tool that knows no boundaries. Not even the lack of a home computer is a problem now that many libraries and other public buildings provide public access. Using a modem connected to any computer, students can talk, research, and share information over telephone lines and on bulletin boards.

You can access the Internet in one of two ways: through an online service, or through an ISP (Internet Service Provider). Online services include many features that aren't accessible unless you subscribe to them; an ISP offers more straightforward access to the Internet including the World Wide Web, news groups, and the Internet Relay Channel (IRC) for live "chats." Before deciding which option is best for your family, do some reading and ask around. Some parents prefer not to turn their children loose on the Internet, so they choose online services that offer "parental control" features. Others equip their computers with software that claims to block access to questionable areas on the Internet. Many books have been written about the Internet and online services, and since our purpose is to provide a very general overview, we won't go into more detail here. (Another reason not to go into greater detail is because the Internet and online services are constantly and rapidly changing. Anything we wrote now might be outdated by the time this book goes to press!)

Three of the most popular online services are America Online (1-800-827-6364), CompuServe (1-800-848-8199), and Prodigy (1-800-822-6922). Through them, users can navigate through hundreds of resource features (*example:* Homework Helper—keyword: Jump Homework). Some bulletin boards have computer programs that can be downloaded, or copied, for home use. To learn more about online services and bulletin boards, visit your local library, check with the media center specialist at your child's school, or contact local computer users' groups. (If you don't know where to start looking for users' groups, ask at a store that sells the type of computer you have at home.)

CAUTION

While many bulletin boards may be accessed for free, most online services charge by the minute. If using an online service also requires a long-distance telephone connection, the costs can add up quickly!

World Wide Web sites which can provide hours of fun and learning for your child are appearing at exponential rates. Following is a list of several worth investigating for children ages 8 and above. You can also ask your child's teacher for recommended sites to explore together.

▸ *Mega Mathematics.* Interactive projects involving map coloring, graphs, knots, and algorithms, presented by the Los Alamos National Laboratory. http://www.c3.lanl.gov/mega-math

▸ *MGBnet/Just for Kids.* Educational projects linked to kids around the world. The site is sponsored by the Missouri Botanical Garden. http://cissus.mobot.org/MBGnet/just_kids.html

▸ *Newton's Apple.* A supplement to public television's program of the same name, this sit, sponsored by Syracuse University, features links to lessons on subjects like movie dinosaurs, hang gliding, earthquakes, garlic, and the Internet. http://ericir.syr.edu/Projects/Newton/

▸ *Science/Math Carnival.* Information about hands-on activities and interactive demonstrations on subjects including air pressure, electricity, infrared cameras, magnetic levitation, and lasers. Sponsored by Sandia National Laboratories/California. http://www.ca.sandia.gov/outreach/html/carnival-intro.html

▸ *Sea World/Busch Gardens Animal Resources.* An encyclopedia of information on animals of all kinds. http://www.seaworld.org/

▸ *Star Child: A Learning Center for Young Astronomers.* A clear, understandable site for learning about space, provided by the High Energy Astrophysics Science Archive Research Center (HEASARC) at NASA. http://heasarc.gsfc.nasa.gov/docs/StarChild/StarChild.html

▸ *The White House for Kids.* A tour directed by Socks the cat includes a history of the mansion, information about children of presidents, and more. http://www2.whitehouse.gov/WH/kids/html/kidshome.html

▸ *Yuckiest Site on the Internet.* Crawling with cockroaches and other insects. http://www.nj.com/yucky/

Ethical issues

Technology use has raised many questions of ethics both old and new. Educator David Thornburg has noted that students can create "shovelware" of their own, pounding out a 300-page tome on virtually any subject by downloading material from the Internet, dressing it up with a few well-chosen images, and pasting on a custom title page. The ethics here are the same as they have always been with research reports: Plagiarism is not scholarship. Following are some tips on ethical issues related to technology use:

▶ It's *legal* to cut-and-paste portions of a copyrighted program, such as a video image, into an original presentation; it's *illegal* to present downloaded information verbatim as one's own writing.

▶ It's *legal* to make one backup copy of a program if it's not included in the original box; it's *illegal* to copy software obtained from another purchaser, or to give copies away of software you have purchased.

▶ It's *legal* to download online freeware or shareware (although shareware authors usually request that you send a small fee).

 **HELP!**

"My child could use a computer to help with composition homework and with research papers. How do I know what to buy?"

Consider buying a computer with a built-in CD-ROM player and word processing software compatible with that used in the school, a modem with a speed of at least 14.4 kilobits per second (k-bps) or faster (28.8 k-bps if you can afford it), and a color printer. If your child doesn't know how to keyboard, a keyboarding program would be helpful, too. Consider also a CD-ROM encyclopedia. If you are not knowledgeable in this area, your best bet is to get advice from someone you know and trust.

"How can I control access to the Internet so that my child doesn't come across objectionable material?"

Information filters are being developed such as LinQ, a combination of hardware, software, and information service (for more information, call 1-800-777-3642). At present, however, there is virtually no way to prevent a bright, determined child from finding something he or she really wants to see. The best way to control your child's access to the Internet is by supervising and monitoring your child's time online, setting firm limitations, establishing clear rules for use, and also establishing (and enforcing) reasonable consequences for violating those rules.

Playing Games

"You can't teach a child unless you reach him."

Unknown

The value of playing games with your child

One of our friends grew up with five brothers and sisters. The expense of raising so many children left little money for movies and other "going-out" activities. Instead, her parents made sure that the house was stocked with games of all kinds—and all of the children grew up to be avid game-players. Although the primary intent may not have been educational, the end results certainly were. Our friend recalls learning how to spell over a *Scrabble* board, learning about money over *Monopoly*, and more while gathered around the table with her family.

The main reason to play games with your child is because it's *fun*. It's a wonderful opportunity for you to spend time together doing something you both enjoy. It's also a ready-made opportunity for you to reinforce basic concepts and skills. In the context of doing homework, games can provide relief from the monotony and drudgery of drill-and-practice. (Almost any child would rather play Hangman than review a written spelling list.) This chapter includes suggestions for dozens of games you can buy or make yourself.* Many can be used to help teach a variety of subjects.

---

* See also the descriptions of recommended software in Chapter 8. Many of these programs use a game format.

"And the winner is. . ."

While recent years have seen the introduction of many non-competitive games (games where "everyone wins"), most still depend on *one* person emerging as winner. When you first play a game with your child that's new to her, it's almost a given that you will be the winner. Parents have asked us whether they should deliberately "lose" on occasion so their children won't be frustrated. We can't in good conscience recommend this. All children would rather win than lose, but most can tell the difference between *really* winning and winning because someone lets them. Instead, try these strategies for leveling the playing field:

1. When playing a game with your child, keep the focus on *self-competition*. Encourage your child to improve his level of achievement each time the game is played. (For example, your child could aim for a higher personal score or a faster time.)

2. Explore several different types of games with your child. Look for one or more that he can eventually play well enough to win. (It's more fun for *you* when your child reaches this point.) You may find that your child has a gift for certain games; we know one third grader who was beating his father at chess by age 6.

3. Don't limit your choices to games of skill. Also include games of chance, where your child has the same likelihood of winning as you do. Young children enjoy *Candyland*, *Chutes and Ladders*, and other games where moves are determined by a spinner or a roll of the dice. These may not be appropriate for homework sessions, since they don't teach much in the way of concepts or skills, but they are fine for other occasions.

When to play games with your child

Naturally you can play games during leisure time "just for the fun of it," but games can also be incorporated into regular homework sessions. For example, instead of doing multiplication flash cards, you can play Multiplication Baseball instead. Draw a baseball field and let your child go from base to base with each fact she gets right. Points are scored for each home run.

▶ In most cases, games should be scheduled for the end of a homework session. ("When you finish all of your other work—neatly and completely—we'll play a game together.") The game can function as the "carrot" at the end of the homework "stick."

▸ If your child is a slow worker, this may not be the best approach. Many teachers permit students to play learning games only after their regular classwork is finished. A child who simply can't get everything done in time feels left out of the fun. You probably can't change the teacher's policy about this, but you can make up for it at home. Divide your child's homework into mini-sessions and play games in between.

▸ Use games frequently to provide the extra drill needed to overlearn information for a test. Children don't mind going over facts again and again if this involves an element of play. (At least, they don't mind as much.)

How to buy games to play with your child

Many commercial games are available through educational suppliers as well as regular toy stores, department stores, and catalogs. Their quality varies greatly. Be sure to examine a game carefully *before* purchasing it. You may not be able to open it if it is sealed, but directions are usually printed on the bottom of the box, and you can use these to determine whether a game is appropriate for your child's needs and skill level. Inquire about the company's return/refund policy at the time of purchase in case a particular game doesn't work out. Here are 12 more questions to guide your buying decision:

1. Does this game reinforce a specific skill or skills my child needs to master?

2. Do I have the time to make an inexpensive game that will do the job as effectively? (If so, stop here and give it a try. If not, continue.)

3. Is the game attractive and appealing in theme, color, and design?

4. Is the game well-constructed and durable?

5. Is the skill level appropriate for my child? (Most games indicate an *age* level—for example, "for ages 5 and up"—but this won't necessarily conform to your child's *skill* level. So this question will take some thought.)

6. Are the directions clear and easy to follow?

7. How long does it take to complete the game? Is it too long or too short to fit the time period I have in mind?

8. How much actual drill-and-practice does the game involve? (Some supposedly "educational" games contain a lot of nonsense or distracting filler activities. These are okay for leisure play, but not for homework sessions.)

9. Does the game enable a child to gauge her own progress in skill development? For example, with a trivia game, a child will know when she is improving.

10. Can the entire game, or parts of the game, be adapted for uses other than those specified by the manufacturer?

11. Is the game simple enough that my child can play it with siblings or friends and without a great deal of help from me?

And, finally:

12. Taking all of these factors into consideration, is the game worth the cost?

As you search store shelves and catalog pages for games appropriate for your child, you may feel overwhelmed by the sheer numbers available. Following are some tried-and-true favorites and newer games that come recommended by parents and children alike. See page 137 for manufacturers' addresses in the event that you can't find these games in stores.*

- ▸ Addition: *Yahtzee* (Milton Bradley); *'SMATH* (Pressman); *Mille Bornes* (Parker Brothers)
- ▸ Making change: *Monopoly* (Parker Brothers)
- ▸ Storytelling: *Spin-a-Story* (Trend Enterprises)
- ▸ Spelling and vocabulary: *Boggle* (Parker Brothers); *Junior Scrabble* (Milton Bradley); *Wordsearch* and *Wheel of Fortune* (both Pressman); *UpWords* (Milton Bradley)
- ▸ Classification: *Pyramid* (Cardinal)
- ▸ General information: *Go to the Head of the Class* (Milton Bradley); *ASAP— The Quick Think Game, Brain Quest, Twenty Questions. . . for Kids,* and *Game of Knowledge* (all University Games); *Outburst* (Hersch)
- ▸ Science: *True Science* (Aristoplay); *The Sierra Club Game* and *Twenty Questions. . . Nature and Science* (both University Games)
- ▸ Geography: *Risk* (Parker Brothers); *Where in the USA Is Carmen Sandiego* (University Games)
- ▸ Strategic thinking: Checkers, chess, Chinese checkers.

When playing these games—and any others you choose—it's important to let your child participate in as many ways as possible. It may seem easier or more efficient for you to keep score or make change, but in the long run your child will benefit more if you let him assume these responsibilities.

---

* Many of the games listed here—including *Monopoly, Yahtzee, Mille Bornes, Scrabble,* chess, and checkers—are also available in versions for home computers.

Manufacturers of Recommended Games

If you can't find games of interest in stores or catalogs, you can write to or call the manufacturers. (When you contact them, request a catalog; you may find descriptions of other games worth considering now or in the future.) In some cases, you can order directly from the manufacturer (after requesting ordering information). In other cases, companies will refer you to stores in your area that carry their products.

- ▸ **Aristoplay**, 334 E. Washington, Ann Arbor, MI 48107; toll-free telephone 1-800-634-7738.
- ▸ **Cardinal Industries**, 21–01 51st Avenue, Long Island City, NY 11101; telephone (718) 784-3000.
- ▸ **Hersch & Co.**, 1900 Avenue of the Stars, Suite 1625, Los Angeles, CA 90067; telephone (310) 553-0900.
- ▸ **Milton Bradley Company**, 443 Shaker Road, East Long Meadow, MA 01028; telephone (413) 525-6411.
- ▸ **Parker Brothers**, 50 Dunham Road, Beverly, MA 01915; telephone (508) 927-7600.
- ▸ **Pressman Toy Co.**, 200 5th Avenue, New York, NY 10010; telephone (212) 675-7910.
- ▸ **Trend Enterprises**, 300 9th Avenue SW, New Brighton, MN 55112; toll-free telephone 1-800-321-5540.
- ▸ **University Games**, 1633 Adrian Road, Burlingame, CA 94010; toll-free telephone 1-800-347-4818.

Games you can make at home

When the cost of a commercial game is prohibitive or unwarranted, when a commercial game is not readably available for a specific skill your child needs to master, or when you decide at the spur of the moment that an educational game would liven up a homework session—then make one yourself! Here are some general guidelines for creating homemade learning games:

1. Don't spend more time making the game than your child will spend playing it. (Depending on the skill it's intended to teach, you may only need to use it once or twice.)

2. Have a specific learning goal in mind. Don't try to incorporate too many goals into one game.

3. Get your child involved in the game-making process. You may want to turn this into a problem-solving activity. ("Let's see, you need to study your states and capitals. How can we make a game of it?")

4. Brainstorm together an imaginative name or theme for the game.

5. Have plenty of materials on hand—scissors, construction paper, cardboard, markers, rulers, and so on. If neither you nor your child is artistically inclined, use magazine, comic book, or coloring book pictures to decorate the game. Stickers and rubber stamps are other creative possibilities.

6. *Write the rules down.* Not only does this avoid future conflict; it also models a writing activity for your child.

7. Don't feel as if you have to make game cards for each and every game. For example, if your child needs to prepare for a science test, just use the questions at the end of the chapter or make up questions based on the text. If your child needs to drill on math problems or reading exercises, use the problems or exercises from the text.

8. Store all learning games and game pieces in your child's study center. Use a plastic dishwashing tub, a milk crate, a tote bag, or a special shelf for keeping odds-and-ends together.

Recommended game formats and suggested ways to play

This section provides some "generic" game formats you can adapt to your child's interests and tailor to skills that need reinforcing. Use your imagination (and your child's) to build these into enjoyable games that meet educational goals. These formats are appropriate for elementary children of all ages; the level of difficulty for each game depends on the content.

We have also suggested several ways to use each game format that teach or reinforce specific skills. Many of these suggestions are interchangeable from one format to another.

Finally, we have provided sample "cards" or "boards" for some games on pages 191–193. You might make copies of several of these, then have them laminated (or cover them with clear contact paper) so they can be written on with erasable crayon and used several times. Naturally, you can also use paper and pencil or chalkboard and chalk for most of these games.

BINGO

Materials needed:

Poker chips, pennies, or squares of paper for space markers
Traditional five-column Bingo cards (see page 191)
Bingo numbers

Rules of play:

1. Call out a question or flash a flash card.
2. If your child provides the correct response, draw a Bingo number, call it out, and have her put a marker on the corresponding space.
3. Play continues until your child gets "BINGO"—five markers in a row either horizontally, vertically, or diagonally.

Ways to play:

- ▶ Learning letters: Write lower-case letters on the Bingo card. Make flash cards of corresponding upper-case letters. (Or do this the other way around.) Show your child a flash card and ask her to match it to a letter on the Bingo board. *Variation*: Have your child match cursive with man-uscript letters.

- ▶ Learning vowels: Label the five columns on the board with A-E-I-O-U rather than B-I-N-G-O. Call out a word. If your child correctly identifies the vowel sound, she may place a marker in any square in that vowel column.

- ▶ Learning sight words: Write vocabulary words in the squares on the Bingo board. Read them aloud, one at a time, and have your child cover each word she recognizes.

- ▶ Learning math facts: Write numerals and math symbols in the squares on the Bingo card. Call out the numbers or symbols ("one," "plus," "divided by") and have your child cover each one she recognizes.

- ▶ Studying science or social studies questions: Write answers on the Bingo board. Read the questions and have your child cover each match.

- ▶ Learning states and capitals: Call out a capital. If your child correctly names the state, draw a BINGO number card and have her cover the corresponding square on the card. (Or do this the other way around: You name the state, and she names the capital.)

TIC-TAC-TOE

Materials needed:

Tic-tac-toe board (see page 192)

Rules of play:

1. Your child is "X" and you're "O."

2. Ask your child a question. If he answers it correctly, he places an "X" on the board. If he answers it incorrectly, you place an "O" on the board.

3. Play continues until one of you gets "Tic-Tac-Toe"—three X's or O's in a row either horizontally, vertically, or diagonally.

Ways to play:

▸ Learning vocabulary: Have your child define vocabulary terms.

▸ Learning grammar: Have your child complete an item in a grammar exercise (*example:* locate a subject or verb in a sentence).

▸ Learning to count: "Skip count" by 2's, 3's, or 4's (or some other number) up to a certain number, then have your child give the next number in the sequence.

▸ Learning to spell: Dictate a spelling word, then have your child write it correctly.

DOTS GAME

Materials needed:

Dots board (see page 193)

Rules of play:

1. Explain that the object of the game is to make squares by joining dots with horizontal and vertical lines.

2. Ask your child a question. If she answers it correctly, she draws a line on the board. If she answers it incorrectly, you draw a line on the board.

3. When a square is completed, the player initials the box and immediately gets another turn.

4. When all squares on the board have been completed, the player with the most initialed squares wins.

Ways to play:

- ▶ Learning consonants: Read a word out loud. Have your child identify the beginning or ending consonant sound.

- ▶ Learning prefixes or suffixes: Show your child a word written on a flash card. Have her identify the prefix or suffix.

- ▶ Learning capitalization and punctuation: Show your child a sentence with a capitalization or punctuation error. Have her identify the error and explain how it should be corrected.

- ▶ Learning Roman numerals: Show your child Roman numerals written on flash cards, and have her identify them.

- ▶ Learning to read maps or graphics: Ask questions about maps or graphics you show to your child.

CONCENTRATION

Materials needed:

Flash cards or playing cards with word or math problems written on one side. Each card must have a match—either a duplicate of the problem, or the answer to the problem. The difficulty of the game will depend on the problems themselves and the number of cards.

Rules of play:

1. Shuffle the cards, then lay them out one deep and upside-down in a square or a rectangle.

2. To take a turn, a player turns any two cards up.

3. If the cards match, the player removes them from the board and immediately gets another turn.

4. If the cards don't match, the next player takes a turn.

5. Play continues until all matches have been made. The player with the most matches wins.

Ways to play:

- ▶ Learning sight words: Make card sets using vocabulary words. Have your child say the word out loud when he finds a match.

- ▶ Learning synonyms *(big-large)*, antonyms *(big-small)*, and homonyms *(blue-blew)*: Make card sets using these kinds of words.

▶ Learning math facts: Make card sets of math problems having the same answer (*examples:* 1 + 5 and 4 + 2, or 6 x 2 and 3 x 4).

▶ Learning the parts of speech: Make card sets of examples and definitions.

▶ Learning map symbols: Make card sets of map symbols or abbreviations and definitions.

CARD GAMES

Materials needed:

Homemade playing cards with words or math problems on one side. Each card must have a match—either a duplicate of the problem, or the answer to the problem.

Rules of play:

1. Follow the rules for Go Fish or Wet Cat (played the same as Old Maid).
2. In the case of Wet Cat, a wild card will be needed.

Ways to play:

You can use your homemade cards to help your child learn the following (among other ideas of your own):

▶ rhyming words
▶ the halves of compound words
▶ vocabulary words and definitions
▶ words and their abbreviations
▶ Arabic and Roman numerals.

HANGMAN

Materials needed:

Paper and pencil or chalkboard and chalk

Rules of play:

1. Explain that the object of the game is to identify an unknown word, starting with only the number of letters.
2. Think of a word, then draw a space for each letter on the paper or chalkboard.

3. Have your child guess one letter at a time. If the letter is included in the "mystery word," write it in the appropriate blank space (or spaces). If the letter is not included in the word, draw a body part in the Hangman. (*Hint:* It's wise to agree ahead of time on which body parts should be included. Sometimes, in an attempt to win, children will want everything to count, from eyelashes to toenails.)

4. To win, your child must identify the mystery word before all the Hangman's body parts are drawn.

Ways to play:

▶ Learning spelling words: Work from your child's test list for that week, and include review words from past weeks.

▶ Learning vocabulary words: Have your child define the word after identifying it.

▶ Learning names of cities, states, and/or countries: Work from the chapters your child is studying in her social studies text, and include review names from past weeks.

MATCH-UPS

Several different formats can be used for matching games. Each requires a different set of materials, but all share the same rules and applications.

Matching Wheel:

1. Cut out a 14" circular piece of cardboard and draw lines dividing it into "pie pieces."

2. Cover the cardboard with clear contact paper.

3. Use erasable crayon to label each pie piece with one-half of a match.

4. Use sticky notes or clothespins to create the other halves of the matches.

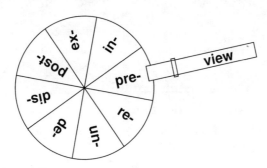

Matching Mini-Puzzles:

1. Write one-half of a match on each side of an index card.

2. Cut the card into two interlocking pieces.

Homemade Dominoes:

1. Divide 2" x 4" pieces of tagboard in two by drawing a line down the middle of each one.

2. On each half, draw a word, symbol, or number.

3. Make sure that each word, symbol, or number is paired with itself at least once and paired with every other word, symbol, or number in the set at least once. Also make sure to include some blanks. Here's an example of what part of a set might look like:

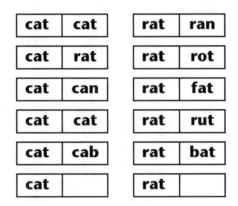

Rules of play, all Match-Up games:

1. Explain that the object of the game is simply to make all the matches correctly, reading them as they are made.

2. To add an element of excitement, have your child do this under timed conditions and try to better his time with each round.

Ways to play:

The possibilities for match-up games are virtually limitless. Types of matches might include:

- ▸ words and pictures representing the words
- ▸ prefixes or suffixes and root words
- ▸ names of land forms ("plateau," "peninsula") or bodies of water ("lake," "inlet") and diagrams or descriptions
- ▸ sentences with missing vocabulary words and the vocabulary words

- numerals and corresponding numbers of dots
- states and abbreviations
- measurement abbreviations and identifications.

SORTING GAMES

Materials needed:

Small slips of paper labeled with the names, problems, definitions, questions, etc., to be sorted

Shoe boxes or small paper lunch bags, labeled and used as containers (for sorting only a few categories)

Egg cartons (for sorting up to 12 different categories)

Rules of play:

1. Explain that the object of the game is simply to sort the items correctly into categories.
2. To add an element of excitement, have your child do this under timed conditions and try to better his time with each round.

Ways to play:

The possibilities for sorting games are virtually limitless. Categories might include:

- long and short vowel sounds
- hard and soft "g" and "c" words (*go* and *age*, *cat* and *face*)
- true and false statements
- animals (vertebrates or invertebrates, warm-blooded or cold-blooded)
- singular and plural nouns.

Making your own board games

You don't have to make board games from scratch to create ones that meet your goals for your child. You can use games you already have if you tie taking turns to answering questions, reading vocabulary words, or solving math problems. It's easy to design your own Reading Pursuit, Math Pursuit, Spelling Pursuit, Social Studies Pursuit, or whatever. If you don't have any board games that you think will work for these purposes, here are some ideas to try:

- Folders from drugstores or discount stores (or office supplies stores) are great for board games. If the folder has a picture on the outside, it can help determine the theme of the game. For example, a folder with a baseball pitcher on the front can become Syllable Strike-Out, and a folder with cats on the front cover can become Capitalization Cat-Nap. Most folders are blank on the inside. Use this blank surface as the game board. Draw a path with crayon or felt-tipped pens, and be sure to include squares with instructions such as *Start, Go Back (1, 2, 3) Spaces, Go Forward (1, 2, 3) Spaces, Free Turn, Finish,* and so on. If the folder has a pocket, use it for storing place markers, rules, game pieces, score pads, and other materials used to play the game.

▸ If your child is a sports fan, draw a football, soccer, or baseball field instead of a regular game board pathway. Your child earns "yardage," "goals," or "base hits" with every correct answer.

▸ Instead of making a traditional square or rectangular game board, cut it in the shape of a favorite cartoon character; a musical instrument; a state, country, or continent; a car or locomotive; and so on.

▸ Science board games can be especially interesting. The path you draw might wind through the human circulatory or digestive system, the solar system, or layer of the earth (from core to crust)—with these serving as the game themes.

▸ Real road maps make excellent game boards, and your child can learn map reading skills simultaneously. If your child is studying a country or a continent in social studies, try to find a map of the place she is studying. Use a felt-tipped pen to draw a pathway between major locations on a city, state, or country map.

▸ Instead of a board, why not use a yard stick or meter stick? With each correct answer, your child can move the marker (a slider or a rubber band) an inch or a decimeter.

You can use homemade board games to test almost anything—from sight words to math facts, spelling words to scientific concepts.

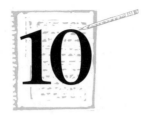

More Resources and Tools You Can Use

"Read, not to contract and confute;
not to believe and take for granted;
not to find talk and discourse;
but to weigh and consider."

Francis Bacon

Recommended reading

Bringing Out the Best: A Resource Guide for Parents of Young Gifted Children by Jacqulyn Saunders and Pamela Espeland (Minneapolis: Free Spirit Publishing, 1991). Written by parents for parents, this book includes information ranging from ways to build a child's self-esteem to tips on dealing successfully with teachers and schools.

Checking Your Grammar by Marvin Terban (New York: Scholastic, 1994). This kids' manual of style covers spelling rules, punctuation, capitalization, contractions, parts of speech, abbreviations, acronyms, and the 100 most often confused and misused words.

Choosing Books for Children: A Commonsense Guide by Betsy Hearne (New York: Delacorte, 1990). Chapters are devoted to selecting different types of books; over 100 titles are recommended.

Classics to Read Aloud to Your Children by William Russell (New York: Crown, 1992). Each selection indicates the age of the child it's suited for and offers suggestions for making a read-aloud session enjoyable.

For Reading Out Loud! by Margaret M. Kimmel and Elizabeth Segal (New York: Dell, 1991). Explains why it's important to read aloud all through the childhood years, tells how to make time to do it, and gives effective ways of reading over 140 suggested books.

The New Read-Aloud Handbook by Jim Trelease (New York: Penguin Books, 1989). Discusses the hows and whys of reading aloud; contains over 300 annotated read-aloud selections.

Playing Smart: A Parent's Guide to Enriching, Offbeat Learning Activities for Ages 4–14 by Susan K. Perry (Minneapolis: Free Spirit Publishing, 1990). Explores photography, cooking, and cultural relativity, journal-keeping and gardening, psychology, and the mental side of physical fitness.

"The Scholastic Homework Reference Series: A Desk Reference for Students and Parents" by Anne Zeman and Kate Kelly (New York: Scholastic). Includes *Everything You Need to Know about American History Homework* (1995), . . . *Math Homework* (1994), and . . . *Science Homework* (1994).

School Power: Strategies for Succeeding in School by Jeanne S. Schumm and Marguerite C. Radencich (Minneapolis: Free Spirit Publishing, 1992). Covers everything students need to know, from how to get organized to how to take notes, study smarter, write better, follow directions, handle homework, manage long-term assignments, and more.

Seven Pathways of Learning: Teaching Students and Parents about Multiple Intelligences by David Lazear (Tucson: Zephyr Press, 1994). Ways to help young people tap into their full learning potential and enrich their lifelong learning in and out of school.

Your Child Can Read Better: A Handbook for Parents by Donna Hartmann and Arlyss Stump (Holmes Beach, FL: Learning Publications, 1980). Background information about reading, with after-school and summer reading activities, games, and gift ideas.

The following publications are available for a nominal fee from the International Reading Association, 800 Barksdale Road, P.O. Box 8139, Newark, DE 19714:

- ▶ "How Can I Encourage My Primary Grade Child to Read?" by Molly Kayes Ransbury
- ▶ "How Can I Get My Teenager to Read?" by Rosemary Winebrenner
- ▶ "How Can I Help My Child Build Positive Attitudes toward Reading?" by Susan Mandel Glazer
- ▶ "How Can I Help My Child Get Ready to Read?" by Norma Rogers

▶ "How Can I Help My Child Learn to Read English as a Second Language?" by Marcia Baghban (this publication has also been translated into Spanish by Ricardo L. Garcia and Rita Maxine Deyoe)

▶ "How Does My Child's Vision Affect His Reading?" by Donald W. Eberly

▶ "What Books and Records Should I Get for My Preschooler?" by Norma Rogers

▶ "What Is Reading Readiness?" by Norma Rogers

▶ "Why Read Aloud to Children?" by Julie M.T. Chan.

Organizations

The following organizations are excellent sources of information for parents as well as teachers.

American Library Association
50 E. Huron Street
Chicago, IL 60611
On the WWW: http://www.ala.org/

Write the ALA to request lists of recommended books for children. For tips on "How to Raise a Reader," go to:
http://www.ala.org/alayou/publications/alaeditions/wlh/raisread.html

International Reading Association
800 Barksdale Road
P.O. Box 8139
Newark, DE 19714
On the WWW: http://www.ira.org/

Single copies of the following brochures are available at no charge from the International Reading Association:

▶ "Eating Well Can Help Your Child Learn Better"

▶ "Good Books Make Reading Fun for Your Child"

▶ "Summer Reading Is Important"

▶ "You Can Encourage Your Child to Read"

▶ "You Can Use Television to Stimulate Your Child's Reading Habits"

▶ "Your Home Is Your Child's First School"

Please enclose a self-addressed, stamped envelope with each mailed request. (Additional IRA publications are listed in "Recommended reading" above.)

National Council of Teachers of English (NCTE)
Order Dept.
1111 Kenyon Road
Urbana, IL 81801
On the WWW: http://www.ncte.org/

Request a copy of "How to Help Your Child Become a Better Writer." For a list of parent and community resources including "Parents' Guide to Literacy for the 21st Century: Pre-K through Grade 5," and "Parents as Writing Partners (7–12)," go to: http://www.ncte.org/parents/list.html

National Council of Teachers of Mathematics (NCTM)
1906 Association Drive
Reston, VA 22091-1593
On the WWW: http://www.nctm.org/

NCTM is primarily an association for educators, but it's worth checking into some of their publications. See especially the "Curriculum and Evaluation Standards for School Mathematics," which helps to explain why teachers may be teaching the way they are.

Reading Is Fundamental, Inc.
Publications Department
600 Maryland Avenue SW
Washington, D.C. 20024
On the WWW: http://www.si.edu/rif/

Copies of the following parent brochures are available from RIF for a small fee:

- ▶ "Building a Family Library"
- ▶ "Children Who Can Read, But Don't"
- ▶ "Choosing Good Books for Children"
- ▶ "Encouraging Young Writers"
- ▶ "Family Storytelling"
- ▶ "Magazines and Family Reading"
- ▶ "Reading Aloud to Your Children"
- ▶ "Reading: What's In It for Teenagers?/Teenagers and Reading"
- ▶ "Upbeat and Offbeat Activities to Encourage Reading"

Tools

On the following 42 pages, you'll find forms, lists, charts, game boards, and more that can help you to help your child with homework. Suggestions for using them are included throughout the book, but don't limit yourself to our ideas. You may find that some of these tools can serve several purposes.

You'll notice that we have included alternate versions of some of the forms. Let your child choose the one he or she likes best.

CERTIFICATE OF
CONGRATULATIONS

TO

_____

DATE

_____

For successfully completing

_____

Good Job!

Keep It Up!

GOOD
WORK!

_____
Signed

How to Help Your Child with Homework copyright © 1997 by Marguerite Cogorno Radencich and Jeanne Shay Schumm. Free Spirit Publishing Inc.

CERTIFICATE OF CONGRATULATIONS

TO

_____

DATE

_____

For successfully completing

_____

_____

Signed

WEEK OF:_____

DATE OF ASSIGNMENT	SUBJECT	BOOK OR PROJECT	PAGE(S)	DATE DUE	GRADE

DATE OF ASSIGNMENT	SUBJECT	BOOK OR PROJECT	PAGE(S)	DATE DUE	GRADE

THE INSTANT (SIGHT) WORDS

Edward Fry

The First 100 Words (approximately first grade)

Group 1a	Group 1b	Group 1c	Group 1d
the	he	go	who
a	I	see	an
is	they	then	their
you	one	us	she
to	good	no	new
and	me	him	said
we	about	by	did
that	had	was	boy
in	if	come	three
not	some	get	down
for	up	or	work
at	her	two	put
with	do	man	were
it	when	little	before
on	so	has	just
can	my	them	long
will	very	how	here
are	all	like	other
of	would	our	old
this	any	what	take
your	been	know	cat
as	out	make	again
but	there	which	give
be	from	much	after
have	day	his	many

The Instant (Sight) Words are reprinted with permission of Edward Fry, Ph.D., Laguna Beach Educational Books. *How to Help Your Child with Homework* copyright © 1997 by Marguerite Cogorno Radencich and Jeanne Shay Schumm. Free Spirit Publishing Inc.

THE INSTANT (SIGHT) WORDS

Edward Fry

The Second 100 Words (approximately second grade)

Group 2a	Group 2b	Group 2c	Group 2d
saw	big	may	ran
home	where	let	five
soon	am	use	read
stand	ball	these	over
box	morning	right	such
upon	live	present	way
first	four	tell	too
came	last	next	shall
girl	color	please	own
house	away	leave	most
find	red	hand	sure
because	friend	more	thing
made	pretty	why	only
could	eat	better	near
book	want	under	than
look	year	while	open
mother	white	should	kind
run	got	never	must
school	play	each	high
people	found	best	far
night	left	another	both
into	men	seem	end
say	bring	tree	also
think	wish	name	until
back	black	dear	call

The Instant (Sight) Words are reprinted with permission of Edward Fry, Ph.D., Laguna Beach Educational Books. *How to Help Your Child with Homework* copyright © 1997 by Marguerite Cogorno Radencich and Jeanne Shay Schumm. Free Spirit Publishing Inc.

THE INSTANT (SIGHT) WORDS

Edward Fry

The Third 100 Words (approximately third grade)

Group 3a	Group 3b	Group 3c	Group 3d
ask	hat	off	fire
small	car	sister	ten
yellow	write	happy	order
show	try	once	part
goes	myself	didn't	early
clean	longer	set	fat
buy	those	round	third
thank	hold	dress	same
sleep	full	fell	love
letter	carry	wash	hear
jump	eight	start	yesterday
help	sing	always	eyes
fly	warm	anything	door
don't	sit	around	clothes
fast	dog	close	through
cold	ride	walk	o'clock
today	hot	money	second
does	grow	turn	water
face	cut	might	town
green	seven	hard	took
every	woman	along	pair
brown	funny	bed	now
coat	yes	fine	keep
six	ate	sat	head
gave	stop	hope	food

The Instant (Sight) Words are reprinted with permission of Edward Fry, Ph.D., Laguna Beach Educational Books. *How to Help Your Child with Homework* copyright © 1997 by Marguerite Cogorno Radencich and Jeanne Shay Schumm. Free Spirit Publishing Inc.

THE INSTANT (SIGHT) WORDS

Edward Fry

The Second 300 Words (approximately fourth grade)

Group 4a	Group 4b	Group 4c	Group 4d
told	time	word	wear
Miss	yet	almost	Mr.
father	true	thought	side
children	above	send	poor
land	still	receive	lost
interest	meet	pay	outside
government	since	nothing	wind
feet	number	need	Mrs.
garden	state	mean	learn
done	matter	late	held
country	line	half	front
different	remember	fight	built
bad	large	enough	family
across	few	feel	began
yard	hit	during	air
winter	cover	gone	young
table	window	hundred	ago
story	even	week	world
sometimes	city	between	airplane
I'm	together	change	without
tried	sun	being	kill
horse	life	care	ready
something	street	answer	stay
brought	party	course	won't
shoes	suit	against	paper

THE INSTANT (SIGHT) WORDS

Edward Fry

The Second 300 Words (continued)

Group 4e	Group 4f	Group 4g	Group 4h
hour	grade	egg	spell
glad	brother	ground	beautiful
follow	remain	afternoon	sick
company	milk	feed	became
believe	several	boat	cry
begin	war	plan	finish
mind	able	question	catch
pass	charge	fish	floor
reach	either	return	stick
month	less	sir	great
point	train	fell	guess
rest	cost	hill	bridges
sent	evening	wood	church
talk	note	add	lady
went	past	ice	tomorrow
bank	room	chair	snow
ship	flew	watch	whom
business	office	alone	women
whole	cow	how	among
short	visit	arm	road
certain	wait	dinner	farm
fair	teacher	hair	cousin
reason	spring	service	bread
summer	picture	class	wrong
fill	bird	quite	age

The Instant (Sight) Words are reprinted with permission of Edward Fry, Ph.D., Laguna Beach Educational Books. *How to Help Your Child with Homework* copyright © 1997 by Marguerite Cogorno Radencich and Jeanne Shay Schumm. Free Spirit Publishing Inc.

THE INSTANT (SIGHT) WORDS

Edward Fry

The Second 300 Words (continued)

Group 4i	Group 4j	Group 4k	Group 4l
become	herself	demand	aunt
body	idea	however	system
chance	drop	figure	lie
act	river	case	cause
die	smile	increase	marry
real	son	enjoy	possible
speak	bat	rather	supply
already	fact	sound	thousand
doctor	sort	eleven	pen
step	king	music	condition
itself	dark	human	perhaps
nine	themselves	court	produce
baby	whose	force	twelve
minute	study	plant	rode
ring	fear	suppose	uncle
wrote	move	law	labor
happen	stood	husband	public
appear	himself	moment	consider
heart	strong	person	thus
swim	knew	result	least
felt	often	continue	power
fourth	toward	price	mark
I'll	wonder	serve	president
kept	twenty	national	voice
well	important	wife	whether

The Instant (Sight) Words are reprinted with permission of Edward Fry, Ph.D., Laguna Beach Educational Books. *How to Help Your Child with Homework* copyright © 1997 by Marguerite Cogorno Radencich and Jeanne Shay Schumm. Free Spirit Publishing Inc.

STORY STUDY GUIDE

Title: _____

Author: _____

About the Setting

Time: _____

Place: _____

About the Characters

_____

_____

_____

_____

_____

_____

_____

How to Help Your Child with Homework copyright © 1997 by Marguerite Cogorno Radencich and Jeanne Shay Schumm. Free Spirit Publishing Inc.

About the Story

The major problem in the story: _____

_____

_____

How the problem was resolved: _____

_____

_____

About the Plot

_____

_____

_____

_____

_____

_____

Vocabulary
Identify and define the most difficult words in the story

_____

_____

_____

_____

STORY STUDY GUIDE

Title: _____

Author: _____

About the Setting

Time _____

Place _____

About the Characters

Give names and nicknames, physical descriptions, personality descriptions

_____

_____

_____

_____

_____

_____

_____

_____

_____

_____

How to Help Your Child with Homework copyright © 1997 by Marguerite Cogorno Radencich and Jeanne Shay Schumm. Free Spirit Publishing Inc.

About the Story

The major problem in the story: _____

_____

_____

How the problem was resolved: _____

_____

_____

About the Plot

(list 5 major events in the story)

_____

_____

_____

_____

_____

Vocabulary

Identify and define the most difficult words in the story

_____

_____

_____

_____

_____

MANUSCRIPT CHART

Zaner-Bloser Style

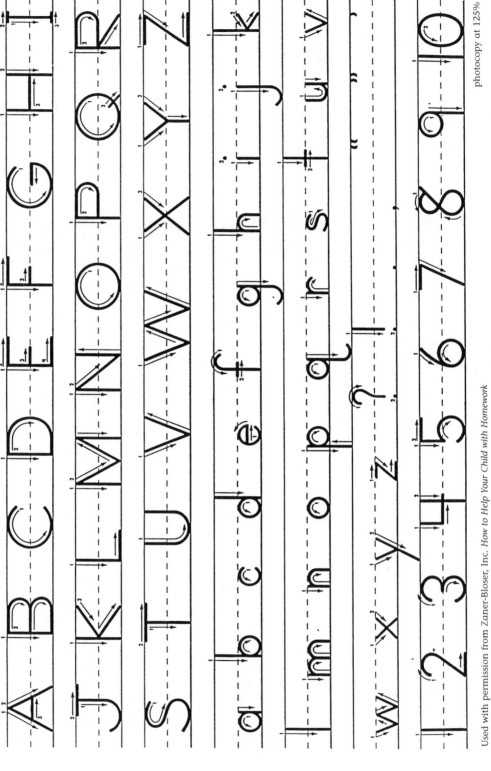

Used with permission from Zaner-Bloser, Inc. *How to Help Your Child with Homework* copyright © 1997 by Marguerite Cogorno Radencich and Jeanne Shay Schumm. Free Spirit Publishing Inc.

photocopy at 125%

MANUSCRIPT PRACTICE PAPER

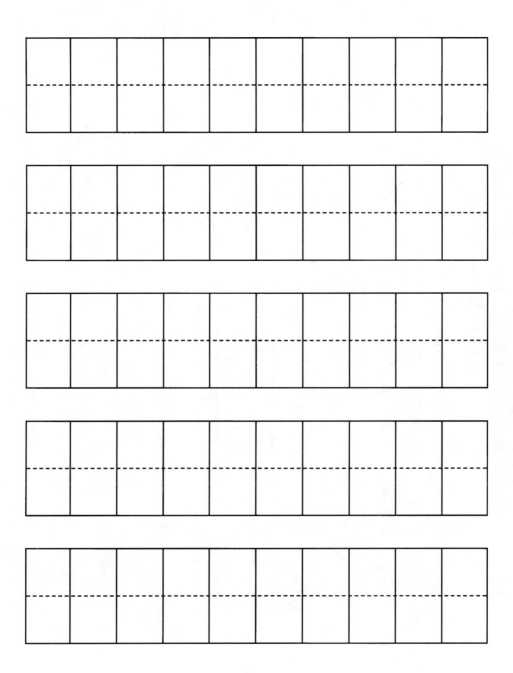

CURSIVE CHART
Zaner-Bloser Style

photocopy at 125%

Cursive Practice — Sample

ate tea lad bad

dab abe cat tad

ace day add rod

eat pea tree fat

life if got dog

age kid ache oh

it kid ski jug

kind take book

late old hill mat

come dime hot end

dim oat toe too pad

tape loop rail air

arm star ask last

tag art ate use

put out you eat

give with own new

hi-ray next first year

eye many too fun

How to Help Your Child with Homework copyright © 1997 by Marguerite Cogorno Radencich and Jeanne Shay Schumm. Free Spirit Publishing Inc.

Cursive Practice Paper

ADDITION TABLE

+	0	1	2	3	4	5	6	7	8	9
0										
1										
2										
3										
4										
5										
6										
7										
8										
9										

MULTIPLICATION TABLE

X	0	1	2	3	4	5	6	7	8	9
0										
1										
2										
3										
4										
5										
6										
7										
8										
9										

SPECIAL PROJECT CHECKLIST

How to Help Your Child with Homework copyright © 1997 by Marguerite Cogorno Radencich and Jeanne Shay Schumm. Free Spirit Publishing Inc.

STEP

DATE
DONE

☐ **1.** Decide on a project theme. _____

☐ **2.** Have theme approved by teacher. _____

THEME:_____

☐ **3.** Make a list of what needs to be done and the order in which the tasks should be completed. (List, then number each task.)

☐ **4.** Decide who is going to do what. (Initial each task.)

☐ **5.** Set deadlines for completion of each task. (Write in the dates.)

TASK	DATE DUE	DATE DONE	PERSON RESPONSIBLE

☐ **6.** Make a list of materials needed to do the project.

☞

☐ **7.** Make a projected budget. (Write the estimated cost of each item.)

TASK	COST

☐ **8.** Send away for resource materials needed.

RESOURCE MATERIAL	DATE REQUESTED	DATE RECEIVED

☐ **9.** Contact community resources.

COMMUNITY RESOURCE	DATE CONTACTED

☐ **10.** Visit the library.

PURPOSE OF VISIT	DATE OF VISIT

☐ **11.** Complete the project ON SCHEDULE.

DATE TURNED IN _____   GRADE _____

SPECIAL PROJECT
AGREEMENT FORM

Today's Date:_____ Due Date: _____

Project Theme: _____

∽

I, _____, agree to do the following tasks by myself.
STUDENT'S NAME

I agree to do them on time.

TASK   **DATE DUE**

_____

_____

_____

_____

I, _____, and I, _____,
PARENT'S NAME   STUDENT'S NAME

agree to do the following tasks together. We agree to do them on time.

TASK   **DATE DUE**

_____

_____

_____

How to Help Your Child with Homework copyright © 1997 by Marguerite Cogorno Radencich and Jeanne Shay Schumm. Free Spirit Publishing Inc.

BOOK REPORT
OUTLINE

I. INTRODUCTION

A. Title of book: _____

B. Author: _____

C. Type of book (example: mystery, adventure, fantasy): _____

_____

D. Setting of book

Time: _____

Place: _____

E. Why I read this book: _____

_____

_____

_____

II. MAIN CHARACTERS

_____

_____

_____

_____

III. SUMMARY OF BOOK

_____

_____

_____

_____

_____

_____

IV. MY FEELINGS ABOUT THIS BOOK

A. The part I liked best: _____

_____

_____

B. The part I liked least: _____

_____

_____

C. This book was (check one)

☐ hard to read   ☐ easy to read   ☐ in between

D. I (check one)

☐ would   ☐ would not

recommend this book to someone else because: _____

_____

_____

How to Help Your Child with Homework copyright © 1997 by Marguerite Cogorno Radencich and Jeanne Shay Schumm. Free Spirit Publishing Inc.

BOOK REPORT OUTLINE
FICTION

I. INTRODUCTION

   A. Title of book: _____

   B. Author: _____

   C. Type of book (example: mystery, adventure, fantasy): _____

      _____

   D. Setting of book

      Time:_____

      Place: _____

   E. Why I read this book: _____

      _____

II. CHARACTERS

   A. Main character (name and description): _____

      _____

   B. Other important characters (names and descriptions):_____

      _____

      _____

      _____

III. SUMMARY OF PLOT

_____

_____

_____

_____

_____

_____

_____

IV. CRITIQUE

A. The part I liked best: _____

_____

_____

B. The part I liked least: _____

_____

_____

C. This book was (check one)

☐ hard to read   ☐ easy to read   ☐ in between

D. I (check one)

☐ would   ☐ would not

recommend this book to someone else because:_____

_____

_____

How to Help Your Child with Homework copyright © 1997 by Marguerite Cogorno Radencich and Jeanne Shay Schumm. Free Spirit Publishing Inc.

NONFICTION

BOOK REPORT OUTLINE

I. INTRODUCTION

A. Title of book: _____

B. Author: _____

C. Subject of book:_____

_____

D. Why I read this book: _____

_____

_____

II. SUMMARY OF BOOK

_____

_____

_____

_____

_____

_____

_____

III. NEW AND INTERESTING FACTS I LEARNED FROM READING THIS BOOK

_____

_____

_____

_____

_____

_____

IV. MY FEELINGS ABOUT THIS BOOK

A. The part I liked best: _____

_____

_____

B. The part I liked least: _____

_____

_____

C. This book was (check one)

☐ hard to read   ☐ easy to read   ☐ in between

D. I (check one)

☐ would   ☐ would not

recommend this book to someone else because: _____

_____

_____

How to Help Your Child with Homework copyright © 1997 by Marguerite Cogorno Radencich and Jeanne Shay Schumm. Free Spirit Publishing Inc.

BOOK REPORT OUTLINE
NONFICTION

I. INTRODUCTION

A. Title of book: _____

B. Author: _____

C. Subject of book: _____

_____

D. Why I read this book: _____

_____

_____

II. SUMMARY OF BOOK

_____

_____

_____

_____

_____

_____

_____

III. NEW AND INTERESTING FACTS I LEARNED FROM READING THIS BOOK

_____

_____

_____

_____

_____

_____

IV. CRITIQUE

A. The part I liked best: _____

_____

_____

B. The part I liked least: _____

_____

_____

C. This book was (check one)

☐ hard to read   ☐ easy to read   ☐ in between

D. I (check one)

☐ would   ☐ would not

recommend this book to someone else because:_____

_____

_____

How to Help Your Child with Homework copyright © 1997 by Marguerite Cogorno Radencich and Jeanne Shay Schumm. Free Spirit Publishing Inc.

BIOGRAPHY

BOOK REPORT
OUTLINE

I. INTRODUCTION

A. Title of book: _____

B. Author: _____

C. Who the book was about: _____

_____

D. Why I read this book: _____

_____

_____

II. WHAT I LEARNED ABOUT THIS PERSON

_____

_____

_____

_____

_____

_____

_____

_____

III. WHY THIS PERSON IS REMEMBERED OR ADMIRED TODAY

_____

_____

_____

_____

_____

_____

IV. MY FEELINGS ABOUT THIS BOOK

A. The part I liked best: _____

_____

_____

B. The part I liked least: _____

_____

_____

C. This book was (check one)

☐ hard to read   ☐ easy to read   ☐ in between

D. I (check one)

☐ would   ☐ would not

recommend this book to someone else because: _____

_____

_____

How to Help Your Child with Homework copyright © 1997 by Marguerite Cogorno Radencich and Jeanne Shay Schumm. Free Spirit Publishing Inc.

BOOK REPORT OUTLINE
BIOGRAPHY

How to Help Your Child with Homework copyright © 1997 by Marguerite Cogorno Radencich and Jeanne Shay Schumm. Free Spirit Publishing Inc.

I. INTRODUCTION

A. Title of book: _____

B. Author: _____

C. Who the book was about: _____

_____

D. Why I read this book: _____

_____

_____

II. SUMMARY OF BOOK

A. What I learned about the person's life: _____

_____

_____

_____

B. What I learned about the person's major achievements: _____

_____

_____

_____

III. PROBLEMS

A. The major problem in the person's life was: _____

_____

B. Here is how this problem was solved: _____

_____

IV. WHY THIS PERSON IS REMEMBERED OR ADMIRED TODAY

_____

_____

_____

V. CRITIQUE

A. The part I liked best: _____

_____

B. The part I liked least: _____

_____

C. This book was (check one)

☐ hard to read   ☐ easy to read   ☐ in between

D. I (check one)

☐ would   ☐ would not

recommend this book to someone else because:_____

_____

_____

How to Help Your Child with Homework copyright © 1997 by Marguerite Cogorno Radencich and Jeanne Shay Schumm. Free Spirit Publishing Inc.

TERM PAPER CHECKLIST

ASSIGNMENT: To write a term paper on _____

_____

DATE DUE: _____

REQUIREMENTS:

My paper will need

☐   a title page

☐   a table of contents

☐   a bibliography

☐   graphics

What kinds of graphics?_____

_____

It should be   ☐   handwritten   ☐   typed   ☐   word processed

STEP	DATE DUE	DATE DONE
☐ 1. Choose a topic	_____	_____
☐ 2. Have topic approved by teacher	_____	_____
☐ 3. Do library research	_____	_____
_____	_____	_____
_____	_____	

How to Help Your Child with Homework copyright © 1997 by Marguerite Cogorno Radencich and Jeanne Shay Schumm. Free Spirit Publishing Inc.

☐   **4.** Contact community resources for information

NAME OF RESOURCE	DATE DUE	DATE DONE
_____	_____	_____
_____	_____	_____
_____	_____	_____

☐   **5.** Write letters to obtain information from national sources

WROTE LETTERS TO

_____	_____	_____
_____	_____	_____
_____	_____	_____

☐   **6.** Take notes

TOOK NOTES FROM THESE SOURCES

_____	_____	_____
_____	_____	_____
_____	_____	_____

☐   **7.** Do an outline   _____ _____

☐   **8.** Write a rough draft   _____ _____

☐   **9.** Proofread rough draft; make corrections   _____ _____

☐   **10.** Write final draft   _____ _____

☐   **11.** Turn final draft in to teacher   _____ _____

BINGO GAME CARDS

	B	I	N	G	O
1					
2					
3			FREE		
4					
5					

		FREE		

TIC-TAC-TOE BOARDS

How to Help Your Child with Homework copyright © 1997 by Marguerite Cogorno Radenich and Jeanne Shay Schumm. Free Spirit Publishing Inc.

DOTS GAME BOARDS

Index

About the Authors

Marguerite Cogorno Radencich, Ph.D., is recognized as one of Florida's foremost educators. Before her death in October of 1998, she was an associate professor at the University of South Florida where she taught graduate and undergraduate courses. She was also an assistant principal and reading supervisor for Miami-Dade County Public Schools.

She published educational software, numerous professional articles, and six books. Most importantly, she will be remembered for her love of reading and as a leader, a mentor, and a friend.

Jeanne Shay Schumm, Ph.D., is a professor and chair of the Department of Teaching and Learning at the University of Miami School of Education. She has coauthored three books with Dr. Radencich, three college education textbooks, and a research monograph on focus group interviews in education and psychology. She lives on the University of Miami campus with her husband, Jerry. As residential masters, they now help college students with their homework.

Marguerite and Jeanne are also the authors of *School Power: Strategies for Succeeding in School* (Free Spirit Publishing, 1992). Jeanne is coauthor of *The Reading Tutor's Handbook: A Commonsense Guide to Helping Students Read and Write* (Free Spirit Publishing, 1999) with her husband, Gerald E. Schumm Jr., D. Min.

Other Great Books from Free Spirit

For children:

How to Do Homework Without Throwing Up
written and illustrated by Trevor Romain
This book features hilarious cartoons and witty insights that teach important truths about homework and positive, practical strategies for getting it done. For ages 8–13.
$8.95; 72 pp.; softcover; illus.; 5⅛" x 7"

For parents and educators:

How to Handle a Hard-to-Handle Kid
A Parents' Guide to Understanding and Changing Problem Behaviors
by C. Drew Edwards, Ph.D.
Packed with practical information and real-life examples, written with authority and compassion, this is a book you'll turn to often for advice, insight, and more on parenting a high-maintenance child. These strategies really work. For parents of children ages 3–12.
$15.95; 232 pp.; softcover; illus.; 6" x 9"

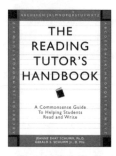

The Reading Tutor's Handbook
A Commonsense Guide to Helping Students Read and Write
by Jeanne Shay Schumm, Ph.D., and Gerald E. Schumm Jr., D. Min.
Based on Jeanne Schumm's years of experience training volunteer tutors, this book is for anyone who wants to make a difference in a young person's life. Includes reproducibles. For grades 1–12.
$18.95; 152 pp.; softcover; 8½" x 11"

Up from Underachievement
How Teachers, Students, and Parents Can Work Together to Promote Student Success
by Diane Heacox, Ph.D.
This step-by-step program helps students of all ages, with all kinds of school problems, to break the failure chain. Students are motivated to succeed because they are part of the team. Includes reproducible handout masters. For parents and teachers of all grades.
$16.95; 144 pp.; softcover; 8½" x 11"

To place an order or to request a free catalog of SELF–HELP FOR KIDS® and SELF–HELP FOR TEENS® materials, please write, call, email, or visit our Web site:

Free Spirit Publishing Inc.
400 First Avenue North • Suite 616 • Minneapolis, MN 55401-1724
toll-free 800.735.7323 • local 612.338.2068 • fax 612.337.5050
help4kids@freespirit.com • www.freespirit.com